ROOMS TO INSPIRE

DECORATING WITH AMERICA'S BEST DESIGNERS

ANNIE KELLY

PHOTOGRAPHY BY TIM STREET-PORTER

RIZZOLI
NEW YORK

The world is but a canvas to the imagination.
—Henry David Thoreau

Rooms to Inspire is dedicated to our mentor, the legendary decorator
Tony Duquette, who was always a great source of inspiration.

Acknowledgments

Our gratitude to all the designers and homeowners—especially Liv
and Glen Ballard—who appear in these pages. Thanks also to
Florence de Dampierre, Martyn Lawrence-Bullard, and Konstantin
Kakanias for their help and advice; Mike Kelly for his technical
support; Christin Markmann; and Jeff Klein for accommodating
us at the City Club while working on this book in
Manhattan. Ashley Hicks kindly let us use a photograph from
his father's archives for the introduction. Sandy Gilbert and
Doug Turshen pulled all of the pieces together so that it made sense.

RIGHT: Inspired by Tony Duquette, Peter Dunham created a
tableau in his sitting room. Family photographs rest on a William
IV painted-mahogany table, which Dunham uses as a desk.
On the wall behind is an eighteenth-century Florentine tapestry.

FOLLOWING PAGE: In his sitting room, Martyn Lawrence-Bullard
displays an eclectic array of objects on an eighteenth-century
limestone chimneypiece—mirror balls from India, a Peruvian
mirror, and Scottish silver-mounted ram horns holding candles.

Contents

Rooms to Inspire

THE INFINITE POSSIBILITIES OF AMERICAN HOME DESIGN

We all need rooms to inspire us. To plan, dream, or search for ideas, it is always fascinating and rewarding to see how other people live. Here we show interiors that were chosen for their inspiring compositions. Their use of color and furnishings, combined with architecture, reflects more than just personal style—they reflect the essence of new American decorating today. These private spaces freely express their designers' sensibilities and inspirations, and hopefully provide useful ideas in the often confusing but creative world of design and decoration. Whether an apartment, a villa, or a country house, the homes profiled in this book, many for the first time, are outstanding examples of today's new decorating trends and ideas.

American houses and apartments come in all shapes, sizes, styles, and price ranges. From Spanish Colonial villas in Los Angeles, to mid-century modern houses in Palm Springs, adobe haciendas in Santa Fe, eighteenth-century colonials in Connecticut, and luxury high-rise apartments in Manhattan, this diverse range of housing styles going back over three hundred years has been influenced by the arrival of each new wave of immigrants from around the world.

As a result, the American design industry has evolved to cater to every taste and regional style. In the last twenty-five years, however, the way Americans decorate and live in their homes has gone through a major transformation. This design revolution has produced smart, stylish furniture and fabrics that can be found at every price range.

It was not always as easy to decorate as it is today, when anything is possible and the furnishings are readily available. Until the late 1980s there were only two options for the consumer. One was to hire a decorator to create a stately home, using furniture and materials unavailable to the general public. If you pick up a copy of the patrician *House & Garden*

magazine from the 1970s and 1980s, you will find page after page of beautifully decorated and timeless houses and apartments. The only other choice was to go it alone with undistinguished mass-market furniture and fabrics, the relics of which can still be seen in second-hand furniture stores; the unsightly, clumsy looking furniture and peeling veneers reveal that the choices at the time were narrow indeed.

The change in American decorating over the last twenty-five years has been chronicled by design magazines that have continuously exposed readers to new and well-designed houses and apartments. This has helped to raise the design stakes. *House Beautiful, Elle Decor, Metropolitan Home*, and other publications use top photographers and skilled layouts to portray the best of American design and decoration. This has encouraged manufacturers of furniture and fabric to create and sell their products for an ever-expanding audience.

Travel abroad does broaden the mind. American taste has also evolved as a consequence of discovering new and exotic locales. From the elegance of an Aman hotel in Asia to intimate cafes in France and the *folklorique* hotels in Mexico, they have all contributed to a demand for more varied and colorful interiors. French and English magazines have played a part, too. *World of Interiors* has been a great inspiration for American tastemakers, introducing them to the old-world charm of run-down English manor houses (which gave rise to the term "shabby chic"), and *Maisons Côté Sud* has inspired countless beach houses in Malibu and the Hamptons. And within the United States, magazines

Tony Duquette designed and built this teahouse at Sortilegium, his property in Malibu, in the 1990s. His love of Asia is apparent, and his use of layered fabric and pattern is particularly successful here. The room demonstrates his belief that good decorating should present a complex image to the eye.

such as *Elle Decor, House Beautiful,* and *Architectural Digest* often feature smart Parisian apartments filled with elegant furniture from the 1940s, which have been a huge influence on current interior design trends.

As early as the 1960s, Crate & Barrel founder Gordon Segal was one of the first to notice the appalling lack of attractive, well-crafted American furniture. He couldn't understand why Americans were able to buy well-designed cars but not furniture. To fill the void, he opened the first Crate & Barrel store in Chicago in 1962, and by the 1980s he had expanded nationally. Ikea, the furniture retail giant from Sweden, began selling in the United States in 1985, and found an enthusiastic market for its modern, well-priced range of furniture and household furnishings. Then, in 1986, Williams-Sonoma bought the Manhattan store Pottery Barn and launched a retail catalogue a year later, offering stylish and fashionable furniture and accessories that have grown in sophistication every year.

Fashion designers also entered the field, the foremost being Ralph Lauren. In the mid-1980s, Lauren opened a flagship store on Madison Avenue in New York, selling furniture, bedding, and accessories, and soon offered design services to the public to help pull it all together. The carefully studied furniture and room settings in the showroom were inspirational and provided accessible ways for homeowners to copy the patrician interiors found in the design magazines. Lauren was soon joined by Calvin Klein, Giorgio Armani, and Isaac Mizrahi, who recently designed a home decor line for Target. Klein and Armani opened stores selling furnishings mostly inspired by Modernism from the 1930s to the 1950s. Now even Gucci sells home accessories. Of particular note was the ice cube tray in the shape of their signature "G," which sold in 2003.

Today, thousands of retail stores have opened to cater to the customer with or without a decorator.

The grand living room at Dawnridge, Tony Duquette's house in Beverly Hills. This is one of his most successful rooms, built around a collection of eighteenth-century paintings that he bought at auction many years ago. He and his wife, Beegle Duquette, designed the chandelier and created the curtain arrangements themselves.

Catalogues pour into our mailboxes, and new websites pop up almost daily offering online almost everything needed to furnish a home, whether you live in Manhattan or Utah.

This increase in travel, both here and abroad, has provided another source of inspiration. Those who have experienced the comfort of stylish hotels have returned home wanting similar amenities for themselves. One of the first of the new breed of fashionable hotels to emerge—and it did seem quite radical at the time—was New York City's Morgans. The French designer Andrée Putman designed this stylish boutique hotel in the mid-1980s. Decorated in subdued grays, the rooms were unique for the emphasis on good design, even down to the choice of wastebaskets. More design-conscious hotels followed, including the Royalton, also in New York, the Delano in Miami, and the Philippe Starck–designed Mondrian in Los Angeles. Another design influence was hotel owner André Balazs's renovation of the Mercer Hotel in New York's SoHo, and then the Standard in Los Angeles, once an inconspicuous retirement hotel on the Sunset Strip, where he created bright, colorful rooms inspired by the 1960s and '70s. Staying in these hotels became a way to experience good bedroom and bathroom design, but it was the concept of total design that was revolutionary in the hotel industry, with every item considered an important part of the room.

The American house has changed too, most noticeably in size. It has become considerably larger, especially with the emphasis today on bedrooms and bathrooms, which can be palatial. Another modern development is that many families are gravitating toward one space—usually the kitchen—which has been expanded to include the dining, living, and entertainment areas; in fact, everything but the bedroom and bathroom. In a way, the American house has come full circle, as this was the way the early pioneers lived—in one all-purpose room, with bedrooms tucked away upstairs.

This living room is a classic example of a patrician interior by the French master decorator Henri Samuel. The colors of the fabrics and the carpet harmonize beautifully with the wood-paneled walls. This kind of decoration is almost inaccessible to anyone without a decorator.

There have been many inspiring decorators in the last hundred years—Elsie de Wolfe, Jean-Michel Frank, Billy Baldwin, and Michael Taylor, to name a few—who have helped define modern American design sensibilities. Fashionable decorating today is currently influenced by the following three designers: Tony Duquette, Billy Haines, and David Hicks.

Tony Duquette was a Californian decorator and artist, and during his lifetime (he died in 1999), he designed everything from houses to opera and movie sets, and remained firmly independent from prevailing trends of Modernism and Minimalism. He loved materials like coral and malachite, and in the 1960s and '70s evolved a flamboyant style that is reflected in the work of many of today's decorators. Duquette was working for the costume designer Adrian when Elsie de Wolfe discovered him in 1940, after she moved to Los Angeles from France to escape the war. De Wolfe was considered the first American decorator, and her instinct to simplify helped strip away the last traces of elaborate Victorian decoration in American interiors. The projects that made her reputation are the design of the Colony Club and the Henry Clay Frick residence (now The Frick Collection) in New York. Then, in 1913, she published *The House in Good Taste*, providing timeless advice.

De Wolfe saw Duquette's extraordinary potential and asked him to make a piece of furniture for her. This began a design collaboration on projects for her clients that lasted until her death in 1950. Duquette worked his entire life in California for private patrons and the film industry but mainly for himself, as he was a compulsively creative person. His legacy is an extraordinary personal style that combined traditional furniture with whatever his magpie eye discovered along the way. He was an enthusiastic entertainer, and most of the cultural and film world of the 1940s, '50s, and '60s crossed his path. His wide variety of clients ranged from the Duke and Duchess of Windsor and heiress Doris Duke, to film director Vincente Minelli and Adrian; he also designed sets for the San Francisco Opera.

In particular Duquette is credited as the costume designer for *Kismet*, and a careful examination of the film reveals his hand in all aspects of its design. Many of the backgrounds as well as the costumes are based on his idealized Asian fantasies. His interpretation of Asian design and architecture fueled his life's work, which could be astonishing in its variety, from rooms to gardens and even churches. Anything that attracted his attention was scooped up, from helicopter landing grids to items found by the side of the road. Who else would claim that his favorite source of inspiration was the Army and Navy surplus auctions at Pt. Hueneme in California's Ventura county?

Actor Billy Haines was Hollywood's number-one box office draw in 1930, but he made a smooth transition to decorating when he lost his MGM contract in 1934. His clients were the great Hollywood stars of the age, including Joan Crawford, Carole Lombard, and Claudette Colbert. He is best remembered, however, for his elegantly modernistic designs. "I loathe cozy cottages," he once said, "They were made for farmers and peasants, not ladies and gentlemen." He began as a Classicist, and loved Chinoiserie and Regency styles, but slowly evolved into a Modernist. Haines worked until his death in 1973, but his Modernist period continues to inspire decorators today. His furniture, designed with clean lines and a hint of Art Deco, can still be found, sometimes with a provenance from specific houses.

The English decorator David Hicks worked in the United States from about 1966 to 1973. He loved America, and was assisted at this time by the now well-known decorator Mark Hampton. During this period, he influenced contemporary American design with his much published work and even designed sheets and towels for textile giant J. P. Stevens. Recently, there has been a big revival of interest in his work; his modern geometric designs combined with both modern and traditional furniture are seen as increasingly chic and iconic. Hicks's ongoing influence is immediately apparent in many of the top

Billy Haines designed this interior in California for one of his favorite clients, who has preserved it almost intact over the years, proving that good decorating is timeless. The blue-and-white color scheme is appropriate for this pool house interior.

decorating magazines, especially his arrangements of the old and the new and the precious with the inexpensive, side-by-side in rooms and on tabletops, in graphic combinations of pattern and color. A visit to Bed Bath & Beyond reveals his influences at work on everyday sheets and bedding. His son, the designer Ashley Hicks, has fueled the revival by reissuing his father's designs for carpet, fabric, and wallpaper. His book *David Hicks: Designer* shows his father's best work, and illustrates the fact, even thirty years later, that good design is timeless.

Today's designers enjoy the best of all possible worlds. Despite the new availability of chic furnishings, they are hardly out of a job; in fact, with America's current obsession for interior design, they have more work than ever. Today their main role is to help homeowners sift through the overwhelming number of decorating choices available, and to create living places that are both comfortable and hopefully inspirational.

In designing your own space, it is tempting to simply reproduce a favorite catalogue or showroom interior, especially when most of us have so little time to pull it all together. However, we would miss the opportunity for personal expression and creativity that make our homes an example of how we would like our own world to look.

In this book, we hope to provide inspiration by showing the creations of designers whose ideas are drawn from both Modernism and today's readily available furniture, or who are inspired by other historical periods. These interiors are often mixed with eclectic finds from flea markets and antiques shops from all over the world to make more personal statements. These homeowners put a variety of elements together in novel and innovative ways that can inspire and sometimes challenge conventional ideas of decorating.

The apartment of Duane and Mark Hampton, who worked with David Hicks for several years in the late 1960s in New York, shows Hicks at his best. He was fearless in his use of color, and designed this apartment as a wedding present for the Hamptons. His combination of antique and modern furniture, as is evident here, is deeply inspirational today.

Hollywood Style

ANNIE KELLY AND TIM STREET-PORTER'S HOLLYWOOD VILLA

About fifteen years ago my husband, photographer Tim Street-Porter, and I bought Villa Vallombrosa from friends who had done much of the original restoration. The villa typifies the element of fantasy for which Hollywood became famous in the 1920s and '30s. With its curved façade and single long window like an exclamation point, it evokes a palazzo in Venice or a small villa in Tuscany.

Villa Vallombrosa overlooks a tiny, hidden valley in Whitley Heights, a residential neighborhood in Los Angeles, developed in the 1920s to recreate the spirit of hillside villages in France, Spain, and Italy. A walk around this picturesque corner of the Hollywood Hills reveals a network of narrow, winding streets and Mediterranean Revival houses, each carefully positioned with a view over its neighbor.

Many of the early movie stars were attracted by the romantic style of this development and came to live here. In 1931, two years after the Villa Vallombrosa was built, Adrian, the costume designer, and his future wife, the movie star Janet Gaynor, moved in. Photographs show the dramatic Hollywood Regency-style decoration of the sitting room, and a memoir by Mercedes d'Acosta mentions an evening that she spent there with Greta Garbo.

From a broad terrace above the street, the front door opens onto a tiny hall with a Gothic arch, from which tunnel-like stairs curve theatrically upward and into the twenty-foot-high sitting room on the *piano nobile*, or main floor. Here, aged ochre colored walls meet the ceiling in a soft cove, giving the room the sensation of limitless height. A carved stone fireplace anchors the room beneath a gilded Louis Philippe mirror flanked by a pair of nineteenth-century sconces.

The villa is essentially one large room that anchors the rest of the house. It is built into the hillside, and at the rear is a central enclosed courtyard with an outdoor fireplace set into the wall on one side. Much of the furniture that we found for the house is French or Italian, and was bought from various antiques shops and auction houses in Los Angeles. However, there is a modern touch in the lack of fussy ornamentation, although after fifteen years there has been a certain amount of layering. The smaller sitting room, for example, owes a lot to the inspiration of the extraordinary Tony Duquette. He suggested and supplied the mirror for this room, to reflect the courtyard garden outside, and the twin pagodas flanking the Empire chest of drawers came from his workshop.

Decorator Tom Beeton was an early source, as quite a bit of the furniture came from his shop on La Cienega Boulevard, while neighbor Martyn Lawrence-Bullard pops in from next door occasionally for a consultation. His has been the most recent influence, and his Ottoman Empire style is gradually creeping in from across the street.

The villa has a rich history. A self-portrait by the fashion photographer Baron de Meyer, taken in front of the sitting room fireplace when he lived here in the 1940s, now hangs in the same room. Another colorful tenant was Edward James, a great patron of Surrealist art, and possibly the model for Sebastian Flyte in Evelyn Waugh's *Brideshead Revisited*, who vanished into a remote corner of the Mexican jungle where he built an inscrutable folly of towers and spires. An example of the enduring Los Angeles preoccupation with creating a fantasy environment, the Villa Vallombrosa lives on in the same spirit in which it was designed.

PREVIOUS PAGE: The living room of Liv and Glen Ballard's Andalusian-style house in Beverly Hills.

RIGHT: The bamboo coffee table was a gift from neighbor and designer Martyn Lawrence-Bullard to add to the Chinoiserie theme of this small sitting room. A collection of small Asian artifacts mingles with Asian-inspired china and transparent glass objects to reflect the light.

LEFT: The palette for the small Chinoiserie-style sitting room ranges from orange to pale purple. The armchairs are upholstered in a gold Fortuny fabric. A nineteenth-century statue of Kuan Yin, the Buddhist goddess of mercy and travel, is surrounded by a display of Japanese Imari plates. The sixteenth-century Dutch painting is in the style of Hans Eworth.

ABOVE: An eighteenth-century secretary desk, which has been in the Street-Porter family since they owned Coveney Manor in England in the nineteenth century, is topped by a Chinese reverse glass painting found in Santa Barbara and flanked by a pair of Chinese ancestor portraits.

ABOVE: The lofty sitting room has a twenty-foot-high ceiling. This tall window overlooking the street is draped by two Indian saris joined together. The furniture is a mixture of eighteenth- and nineteenth-century French and Italian antiques.

RIGHT: An embroidered textile from Tony Duquette acts as a backdrop on the sitting room wall. Eighteenth-century French armchairs feature a playful mix of fabrics; the pink and white striped silk is from the Silk Trading Company.

ABOVE: The sitting room chimneypiece is original to the house. Echoing its rocaille motif is a nineteenth-century French gilded mirror above and a pair of ormolu sconces on either side. The footstool is upholstered in Fortuny fabric. The pale palette of the fabrics used here reflects the purposely distressed wall color.

RIGHT: A small unframed early-nineteenth-century French portrait rests for the moment on an eighteenth-century Italian chair bought from decorator Tom Beeton.

ABOVE: On a small table opposite the bed in the master bedroom, a tableau of objects includes a vase of flowers from the garden. A Directoire sofa on the opposite wall provides a comfortable seat.

RIGHT: Popsy the cat has claimed a French Empire chair in front of the four-poster bed in the master bedroom. The Fortuny-style wallpaper is from Clarence House.

CLOCKWISE FROM TOP LEFT: Surrounded by a halo of Japanese Imari plates, a wooden polychrome statue of the goddess Kuan Yin presides over a corner of the sitting room.

An eighteenth-century portrait is flanked by a pair of crystal girandoles on top of an Empire chest of drawers in the small sitting room.

A personal collection of glassware and religious objects in the large sitting room includes a reliquary cross from France.

A corner of the eighteenth-century Georgian secretary desk that Tim Street-Porter inherited from his parents holds a silver goblet that belonged to his grandfather.

A Mexican equipal table provides an eclectic note to the living room.

The crystals on this nineteenth-century tole candelabra reflect the light in the living room.

Modern Andalusian Revival

LIV AND GLEN BALLARD'S FAMILY HOUSE IN BEVERLY HILLS

Once a city of style and elegance, Beverly Hills has fallen prey to developers, and many of its best houses from the 1920s and 1930s have been torn down and replaced with awkward and overblown mansions. Although it may be too late to save its once graceful residential neighborhoods, individual houses are being rescued and preserved, like this Andalusian-style house designed by Roy Seldon Price in 1928.

When owners Liv and Glen Ballard found this house, it had survived one restoration relatively intact, and I was brought in to help them furnish it. Glen is nothing if not contemporary: a songwriter and producer with five Grammy wins plus nominations for Academy and Golden Globe awards, he and Liv wanted the house furnished with a modern sensibility without compromising its architectural heritage.

Hidden from the street by a high wall, with a Moorish garden in front designed by Tichenor & Thorpe, the house turns in on itself, Andalusian-style, creating a private and serene world of interlocking rooms and courtyards. Glen describes it as "like living inside a beautiful conch shell."

The front door, defined by big yellow oil jars, opens into a cool tile-lined entry space. The interiors are distinguished architecturally by a rich vocabulary of deeply set niches, arches, beams, moldings, beautifully plastered walls, and dramatic spaces. We kept the house spare of extra ornament, painting everything white

as a backdrop for the Ballard's growing collection of strong pieces of furniture and to give the house a light, contemporary feel. The house spoke so eloquently that Liv and I worked together on what became a shared passion.

From the entry, stairs descend to the living room with an end window, where we built a Moroccan-style daybed, framing a view of the fountain in the swimming pool. The large fireplace provides another focus in the room which, with very little detailing, appears almost modern in its severity. Hung above it is a Peruvian Madonna, to emphasize the house's Spanish roots. The furniture was kept low and comfortable here so as not to interrupt the flow of space. As Glen is a musician, this room is designed to seat a crowd of people comfortably around the piano.

Leading from this room is the library, with a cement floor that we edged in pebbles. The fireplace was missing its original screen, so we copied a seventeenth-century screen from La Miniatura, the Frank Lloyd Wright house in Pasadena that I had renovated several years earlier. The sofa and armchairs here are upholstered in a fabric from Robert Kime, an English

A white linen Christian Liagre sofa anchors the sitting room; its low design was chosen to keep the view open from one end of the house to the other. The author designed the upholstered bench, which doubles as a coffee table.

fabric designer whose inspiration is ancient textiles from Europe and the Middle East. From the Moroccan daybed in the living room, the view up the stairs forms a continuous sight line back through the entry, the dining room, and beyond to a small colorful breakfast room. I designed the dining table using a griffin motif picked up from the house's original window bars, which are visible in the next room. The French Neo-Gothic dining chairs were discovered in Sydney, Australia. Lighter in appearance than the usual Spanish equivalent, they suited the room's delicate proportions. Next to the living room is an enclosed courtyard. Here, we added a fireplace, and renovated a small fountain decorated with blue antique tile. This area was repaved with a terracotta floor tile carefully matched to similar original tiles from the dining room floor, to give better visual indoor-outdoor continuity.

The kitchen has dramatically high ceilings: there is even a small upper window that opens into it from the second floor. It was reworked from the previous renovation—the cabinet doors were upgraded, for example—but the practical layout was kept intact.

The basement, reached via an archway and stairs from the main living room, was where the greatest transformation took place. Architect Michael Mekeel was brought in to help create a wine cellar, tasting room, and gym out of a long-existing storage area.

Upstairs, the bedrooms enjoy palm tree vistas of Beverly Hills. The master bedroom was created by two spaces joined together. The first, a towerlike volume, houses a four-poster bed hung with white linen to create an intimate and cozy space within a space. The second area was designed as a small living room to offer a retreat from the more public rooms below.

This beautiful house needed very little alteration to make it comfortable; it has just as many amenities as its overblown neighboring mansions and a million times more charm and style.

The long Moroccan daybed was designed to fill the window alcove at one end of the sitting room. A pair of French Gothic chairs and two nineteenth-century French chairs from Indigo Seas round out the seating arrangement. The exotic lamps are from Fortuny.

ABOVE: In the corner of the sitting room, the Moroccan daybed has been paired with a Turkish stool and matching Moroccan chair.

RIGHT: Lit by a Fortuny lamp and upholstered with cushions of Fortuny fabric, a nineteenth-century Indian inlaid settee stands against one wall of the sitting room. In the German Rococo mirror above can be seen a Spanish Colonial Cuzco-style painting of a Madonna that reinforces the house's Spanish heritage. A silver tray of votives rests on the floor.

ABOVE: The breakfast room is filled with a combination of sunny yellow and warm red furniture. The tile floor is original to the house.

RIGHT: The French Neo-Gothic chairs were found in Sydney, Australia, and are a perfect match for the dining table designed by the author. The curves of the nineteenth-century European chandelier above echo the table's wrought-iron base. Spanish Colonial Casta paintings on the wall provide a link to the house's origins.

ABOVE: An armchair and footrest covered in fabric by Robert Kime, created after an antique textile design, stand in front of a Syrian mirror in the library. The fireplace grille was based on a seventeenth-century version found at Frank Lloyd Wright's house La Miniatura, which was also decorated by the author.

RIGHT: A white linen sofa from the Fainting Couch rounds out the library seating. The two pillows by Brigitte Singh were found in Paris; a striped silk bolster adds a graphic counterpoint.

ABOVE: In the upstairs master bedroom, a cozy sitting area features a bench upholstered with Indian fabric surrounded by a sofa and armchairs in white linen from Diamond Foam and Fabric. The antique cushions on the sofa are from Indigo Seas.

RIGHT: The master bed, flanked by a pair of Moroccan chairs, was designed by the author and hung with delicate white linen. Its height was planned to make the high bedroom ceiling seem more intimate in scale. The bedding is from Chelsea Textiles.

Movie Star Glamour

MARTYN LAWRENCE-BULLARD'S VILLA IN THE HOLLYWOOD HILLS

It seems only natural for Martyn Lawrence-Bullard to live in Hollywood. Drawn to glamour all his life, he moved from London to Los Angeles to become an actor, but soon found that decorating houses was more exciting than the tedium of movie sets. Here, Lawrence-Bullard set up the design company Martynus-Tripp, which has now become Martyn Lawrence-Bullard Designs.

Lawrence-Bullard's house is in the Hollywood Hills in picturesque Whitley Heights, where it is easy to imagine that you are back in the early 1920s and might catch a glimpse of onetime residents like Maurice Chevalier, Gloria Swanson, or perhaps even Bette Davis, sweeping past in their Duesenbergs. This suits Lawrence-Bullard, as it is exactly how he imagined life here when he was still living in cold, gray London.

The house has its own Hollywood stories: William Faulkner tapped away at a typewriter on the upstairs balcony, keen to escape the studios, but Lawrence-Bullard decided to call it Villa Swanson, in honor of the actress who moved there to shoot *Sunset Boulevard*. Who could blame him? Gloria Swanson was much more photogenic.

He sensibly refused to change much when he bought it. Not the least of its charm is the jumble of Mediterranean-style rooms that nestle into the sloping garden behind the house. The villa opens directly onto the street. A heavy wooden antique door set in a white stucco wall opens to reveal a richly decorated courtyard and tiled veranda. Inside, Lawrence-Bullard painted the thick plaster walls white, stained the floors a deep brown, and painted the doors glossy black. The main living rooms follow the curve of the street outside. They are decorated using a rich mixture of reds, whites, and blacks, textures, and fabrics with an exotic Middle Eastern influence; the emphasis is on luxury and comfort in a relatively small space. Large white upholstered furniture blends in with the white walls to give the long narrow rooms a greater feeling of depth.

While Lawrence-Bullard retained the spirit of the house in his use of antiques, a crisp choice of colors helps keep it fresh and contemporary. There are two dining areas. The first, at the end of the living room, is hung with a chandelier of Lawrence-Bullard's design, influenced by the legendary designer Tony Duquette. The second is the original dining room, which is filled with nineteenth-century ebony-and-ivory inlaid furniture. Bell-shaped Turkish glass candleholders on the crystal chandelier deepen the sense of exoticism.

Lawrence-Bullard retained the kitchen's original charm, upgrading it with marble countertops. A small dining alcove, filled with a striped bench seat of his own design, is the perfect place for an early morning breakfast.

Upstairs off a small landing and tucked into the hillside, is a pocket-sized guest bedroom furnished in red toile. It feels larger than it is because Lawrence-Bullard used the same fabric throughout, which unifies the space and gives a sense of comfort and luxury.

A stucco staircase winds up to a movie-star bathroom in original condition, with walls of mirror and black-and-yellow tile, and the master bedroom which holds a commanding position over the cul-de-sac below. This room continues the exotic atmosphere with an ornate Portuguese bed laden with Lawrence-Bullard's collection of fabrics, picked up on many trips to Istanbul and France. Today, the house has the atmosphere of a piece of the early nineteenth-century Ottoman Empire that has unexpectedly landed in Los Angeles.

Author William Faulkner once used this upstairs balcony at the Villa Swanson to write, preferring this peaceful alcove to an office at the nearby Hollywood film studios. At night, the Turkish incense burners are used as candleholders to add romantic lighting to the master bedroom. The street entrance opens onto the antique tiled courtyard below. The main living room can be glimpsed through the red silk curtains.

ABOVE: Martyn Lawrence-Bullard had his family crest hand-painted on the backs of these nineteenth-century ivory-inlaid ebony chairs. A collection of books and Roman marble statuary sits on the matching inlaid ebony dining table. The chandelier, which was original to the house, hangs from a stenciled beamed ceiling above.

RIGHT: A close-up of the dining room chandelier shows that Lawrence-Bullard has added hanging incense burners from Istanbul. Two silver Pugin candlesticks rest on the dining table. A Malibu tile fountain can be seen through the silk curtains.

The white linen
furniture combined
with white walls
form a neutral
backdrop for a rich
mixture of fabrics and
textiles in the main
living room. On the
Lawrence-Bullard-
designed coffee
table are displayed
a collection of ivory
and penwork boxes.
An eighteenth-century
Italian family portrait
hangs above a
seventeenth-century
Portuguese chest
of drawers.

ABOVE: Red linen armchairs and a seventeenth-century French chair surround a small dining table in the living room. The Lawrence-Bullard chandelier was inspired by the work of designer Tony Duquette. A pair of eighteenth-century Dutch mirrors flanks the entry to the dining room.

RIGHT: This nineteenth-century ebony and ivory desk was bought in London. A portrait by French artist Henri Gascar leans casually on the top. Mirrored balls, which reflect the light, help brighten up a dark corner of the main living room.

ABOVE: The Portuguese master bed is decorated with pillows sewn from a collection of nineteenth-century Scottish paisley fabrics. The sheets are from Pratesi.

RIGHT: The bed in the guestroom has a carefully composed selection of matching fabrics. This petite room has been upholstered with red Chinoiserie toile fabric from Old World Weavers, which includes the bed corona. The nineteenth-century French faux bamboo furniture was found at 1stdibs.com.

CLOCKWISE FROM TOP LEFT: On the first-floor landing, a nineteenth-century Indian polychrome table is full of eclectic objects; above it is an eighteenth-century Venetian mirror in the Turkish style.

The wall of a breakfast alcove in the kitchen is hung with Mexican retablos. Lawrence-Bullard designed the built-in settee behind the Indian ivory-inlaid table.

An eighteenth-century Italian olive wood prayer chest by the staircase holds a collection of sculpture, including a second-century Roman hand that has been transformed into a candelabra.

A Syrian chair stands next to a period stove in the kitchen. Lawrence-Bullard removed the original cupboard doors to display his collection of French apothecary and confectionary jars.

The fireplace in the master bedroom has been stenciled by artist Kelly Holden to match a piece of paintwork found on the hearth.

A stenciled ceiling adds a note of interest on the first-floor landing. The alcove holds a seventh-century Hellenic drinking vessel, a fifteenth-century Italian terracotta mask, and a small Roman glass bowl from the collection of designer Tony Duquette.

A Confident Sensibility

MARIAN McEVOY'S RETREAT ON THE HUDSON RIVER

When Marian McEvoy was editor-in-chief of *Elle Decor* and then *House Beautiful*, both magazines crackled with inspiration. Her strong, distinctive style encouraged decorators and designers to be as creative as possible, and this attitude is reflected in her own house on the Hudson River in upstate New York. The restored eighteenth-century building, with its stunning view over the river, dazzles with a wealth of color, ideas, and charm.

Nothing is bland about McEvoy's taste, influenced by a long stint in Paris as a fashion editor for both *Women's Wear Daily* and *W* before she began her career in the New York design world (she now produces books—her most recent is *Glue Gun Decor: How to Dress Up Your Home—From Pillows and Curtains to Sofas and Lampshades).* Her house embodies her skill in applied decoration. As a teenager, she was inspired by Tony Duquette's freedom and experimentation with design, and with the same confident sensibility, she has made this house her own personal canvas. The furniture has been carefully edited. McEvoy moved from a much larger place in the country several years ago, and was surprised how much of it could fit into this house. The small three-story house was based on an original eighteenth-century stone foundation, while the upper floors are new.

Originally an inn reached by the river, this house has been reincarnated as the hospitable center of McEvoy's large circle of friends. Planned for entertaining, each corner has been carefully thought out. The living room has been designed to comfortably seat ten to fourteen people, and the dining room eight. In the summer, however, all of McEvoy's entertaining takes place on the large porch that overlooks a picture-perfect view of the river, so that even more friends can be squeezed in.

A great advocate for recycling furniture, she correctly insists that "sofas can be a lifetime thing," and she re-covered a pair of them in white to act as a backdrop for a living room rich with applied designs. The two facing sofas are book-ended by two pairs of chairs. Flanking the fireplace is a pair of "cartoon Baroque" Spanish chairs found at auction, upholstered in white linen. McEvoy outlined them in red trim, and with a careful use of her favorite glue gun, appliquéd cut-out designs from a Suzani textile. The white fireplace has been outlined with a black pen, giving it the look of a Roy Lichtenstein painting.

Upstairs, in the master bedroom, McEvoy's bed is a masterpiece of applied shellwork, framed by an ebonized headboard. The room has a graphic color palette of yellow, white, and black that is both rigorous and completely feminine. Yellow painted wall panels defined by black tape are an incredibly simple way of adding structure to the room.

Downstairs, in the basement, which retains the original eighteenth-century stone walls, McEvoy has installed her extensive design library. The mood is cozier here: tables are piled high with books, and a nineteenth-century French sofa is covered with cushions McEvoy has appliquéd from her collection of cut-up Suzani textiles discovered on eBay.

Marian McEvoy reworks her existing furniture rather than replacing it each time she moves. Here, she reupholstered her living room sofa in white linen with a contrasting cord to provide a backdrop to her creative designs with fabric. A print of tulips hangs on a square of pink wall above, defined by glued-on strips of black tape.

PREVIOUS PAGES: In the living room, two Italian chairs with white seats and backs outlined by red braid flank an Italian table. The lampshade has been hand-painted in red rectangles lined with black braid. The etched glass pictures along the stairs in the background are by Suzan Etkin.

The library retains its original eighteenth-century walls. McEvoy created the three collages below the shelves of books using a collection of autumn leaves. Pillows decorated with cut-out Suzani textiles fill the comfortable daybed.

RIGHT: In the living room, a pair of "cartoon Baroque" Spanish chairs bought at an auction have been decorated with cut-out Suzani textiles appliquéd using McEvoy's trademark glue gun. The white-painted andirons were found locally.

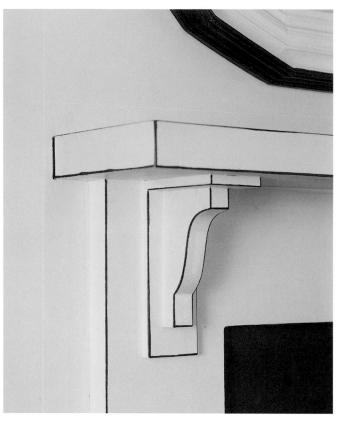

CLOCKWISE FROM TOP LEFT: Small framed groups of shells decorate a wall in the master bedroom.

The white living room fireplace has been graphically outlined in black pen.

Another corner of the master bedroom shows McEvoy's masterful black-and-white theme.

The walls in the master bedroom have painted yellow panels defined by black tape.

RIGHT: The desk in the master bedroom features lamps found on eBay that relate to the graphic curves of the intricate shell mirror on the wall.

In the Swim

FLORENCE DE DAMPIERRE REBUILDS A FAMILY POOL HOUSE

For many people, a pool or guesthouse is a golden opportunity to take a few chances with decorating, or to be creative while continuing the theme of the main house. Following the tradition of fantasy pavilions in the garden, author and decorator Florence de Dampierre decided to rework her existing pool house.

A creation of the 1970s, it had nothing to do with the patrician eighteenth-century main house. After several years of living in the fine old Litchfield, Connecticut, house in the center of town that she shares with her husband, Sean Mathis, she designed a Palladian-style pavilion with two wings that linked it stylistically with the main house. "On one hand I carried on the same theme," explains de Dampierre. "The woodwork both inside and out relates to the main house, but on the other hand its whimsical quality is based on some of the great follies in Europe."

While her exuberant sense of color is already evident in the original house, here she decided to experiment even more, bringing the vibrant colors of summer to a building little used in winter. "I love color and do think it is very important in decorating," says de Dampierre, "and I wanted the pool house to be cool and peaceful."

She designed the voluminous main room with a proportionately scaled eighteen-foot-high ceiling, from which she suspended a large pagoda-style lamp. At the rear of the space, a kitchen provides plenty of room for summer meals, and is separated from the main space by a serving table. De Dampierre found

an eighteenth-century soapstone sink that she resealed and installed in the green poured concrete counter-tops. The shelving throughout, inspired by Chinese Chippendale furniture, has been given a background splash of bright green that unifies this large multi-purpose room.

The living room is anchored by a pair of comfortable sofas slip-covered in white linen, which face a substantial stone fireplace. De Dampierre painted the floors white throughout and stenciled them with a geometric green border. To keep the interiors bright, she used glazed French doors as interior doors on one side of the main room. They separate a Chinoiserie-style billiards room with antique-style wallpaper from a bright green dining room, which repeats the green of the living room shelving.

In this pool pavilion, summer is very much the theme. Nineteenth-century English wildflower prints hang on the walls, and flowers also appear on the curtain fabric and are inset on the seats of the dining room chairs. And on a sunny day, when the French doors to the pool terrace are all open, the room embraces the garden.

The living room in the pool house is a careful composition of color and pattern. The bookcases contain prints and objects with a water theme, and three works by Lebanese artist Nabil Nahas. The fabric draped over the sofa is from Portugal. Florence de Dampierre designed the ottoman that doubles as a coffee table.

The kitchen end
of the pool house
was designed
for entertaining,
with a French
Laclanche stove
and poured concrete
countertops.
De Dampierre uses
it to host casual
lunches as well
as parties. The
fresh green shelving
runs throughout
the room, unifying
its different areas.
A rich green
also covers
the comfortable
wing chair.

ABOVE: A good pool house should have a pool room. Here, antique Chinese bamboo chairs and Chinoiserie-style wallpaper from Schumacher combine with a nineteenth-century billiards table to create an exotic atmosphere.

RIGHT: The bright green color scheme of the pool house explodes onto the walls of this dining room. The nineteenth-century English wildflower prints on the walls, the floral curtain fabric, and chairs from Crate & Barrel link this room to the large garden outside. De Dampierre designed the dining table to resemble a tree trunk.

New York Flair

MURIEL AND NUNO BRANDOLINI'S EXOTIC TOWNHOUSE

In this Upper East Side terrace house, decorator and designer Muriel Brandolini has created an exotic hothouse atmosphere in a strong personal manner. Brandolini has a very sophisticated European sensibility, but is also deeply influenced by her childhood in Vietnam. Here, she has married the two influences with style and flair.

Brandolini says that she usually follows her instincts, but the colors she works with depend on the tastes of her clients as well as the overall aesthetic of the project.

Inside the front door, a small library expands from the entry hall. A seating arrangement around a white marble fireplace creates a kind of vestibule, a place to sit before entering the rest of the house. Low armless sofas are upholstered in a mix of antique Asian fabrics on velvet. Piles of reference books fill the shelves, evidence of the extensive research Brandolini does before she embarks on a new project. When she is at home, Brandolini works in this room partially hidden behind a small nineteenth-century French screen, at a desk overlooking the street, which is visible through a thicket of green ferns.

The library space is lined with dark green corduroy fabric, with moldings painted a darker green; a contrasting white ceiling elevates the space. The white mats around the photographs that line the dark green walls echo this. Here, as throughout the house, the stained wood floor is kept a pale gray.

From here, a watery green-painted passage leads into a large living room overlooking a small garden edged distinctively with tall bamboo. Three main elements anchor the room. The most noticeable is a colossal beaded chandelier shaped like a ship, which seems to sail across an imaginary sea overhead. On the left wall, a large painting by New York artist Ross Bleckner gives the room a floating quality, as the green abstract shapes look like giant bubbles. The third element is

a comfortable overscaled red sofa, which sits below windows hung with beautiful, transparent Chinese-style blinds. Brandolini edged the room's moldings in yellows and greens, and painted the walls an indefinable pale purple-gray reminiscent of butterfly wings. The room's fantasy elements are grounded by a glossy modern fiberglass coffee table from Mattia Bonetti's "Smarties" series of furniture.

Downstairs, in the basement kitchen, gray zinc cabinetry harmonizes with stainless steel appliances. The drama here comes from the modern chandelier by Ingo Maurer, designed in wire and suspended personalized sheets of paper that seem to explode in the room. Brandolini has hung it with family drawings and snapshots. The chandelier hangs over a 1940s marble table.

Leading from this room back toward the garden is a dining room as rich as a padded jewel box. The walls are of hand-embroidered silk, and half of the room is given over to a huge nineteenth-century daybed piled high with exotic fabrics and cushions. A long contemporary dining table fills the rest of the space, surrounded by nineteenth-century inlaid ebony dining chairs upholstered in rose pink Fortuny fabric. Brandolini has confidently painted the woodwork purple and the ceiling an off-white. She explains her entertaining style: "I have no specific formula for my entertaining, but my constants are a beautifully set table and fresh flowers." Brandolini adds, "The walls of my dining room are hand-embroidered with motifs reminiscent of my childhood in Vietnam and convey a feeling of elegance and coziness."

In the living room, a slipper chair by Muriel Brandolini and a nineteenth-century armchair flank a console by Hjort, designed in the 1920s. A whimsical chandelier in the shape of a ship by Claire Cormier-Fauvel floats in front of a colorful painting by Ross Bleckner.

A large red nineteenth-century sofa anchors the living room. The "Smarties" coffee table designed by Mattia Bonetti provides shine and creates scale for the room. Underneath, the wool Caleydo rug by Fedora Design links the yellows in this colorful space. The exotic window shades are from Lilou Marquand.

Upstairs, the airy main bedroom is filled with light. With a high ceiling, it overlooks the rear of the house, and, despite being in the midst of Manhattan, it is quiet and peaceful, well-insulated from the traffic by the row of opposing townhouses on the other side of the garden. A dramatic tole chandelier hangs from the ceiling over the silk-damask upholstered bed. The room's colors are subtle and peaceful: blues, silvers, and the pale coffee tint of the straw fabric that lines the walls. A bright pink Victorian chair upholstered in Chinese embroidered silk provides contrast. Brandolini designed the main bathroom to be entirely padded with her own fabric, lit by a shell chandelier. "My inspiration rarely comes from anything concrete, such as travels, books, or art, but rather it stems from my vivid imagination," Brandolini explains.

This bathroom is shared by a guest bedroom, which doubles as a family media room. Shelves filled with books, DVDs, and videos, in neat order, surround half the space and look almost like wallpaper. A screen descends from the ceiling, which has been lined with long strips of patterned Brandolini fabric. The other two walls are finished with straw in geometric rectangles, over which Brandolini has hung various artworks so that each wall becomes a composition. The nineteenth-century metal bed is piled high with crisp white linens and faces a pair of painted Neoclassical chairs and a Chinese coffee table at the other end of the room. Brandolini chose a carpet with a vivid burst of color— yellows, reds, and purple on a black background—to add an even richer layer to this intense space.

On the top floor, with the best light and views, are the children's bedrooms. Fillipa's room is a cheerful space in pinks and pale greens, with a lacquered silver bed. Her pink and green carpet is modern and feminine. Brando's room is more grown-up. His modern desk by Martin Szekely dominates the space, which is upholstered with more Brandolini fabric in a masculine geometric pattern.

In the dining room, a late-nineteenth-century settee is a comfortable place to retire after a meal. The pillows are made from Brandolini's collection of vintage fabrics from Turkey, Japan, and China. Mid-nineteenth-century French chairs surround the dining table. The walls are upholstered with hand-embroidered Vietnamese silk.

ABOVE: Turn-of-the-century painted armchairs face each other across a coffee table laden with books in the media room, which also functions as a guest bedroom. The nineteenth-century wrought-iron bed rests on a Coral rug by Fedora Design.

RIGHT: The master bathroom is lined with Brandolini fabrics. The sink, bathtub, and toilet have been kept a plain white to keep the focus on the walls. The white shell chandelier is by Cormier-Fauvel.

PREVIOUS PAGES: The bed in the master bedroom is upholstered in eighteenth-century French fabric and made up with hand-embroidered linens. The eclectic collection of artworks on the wall behind it include a painting by Philip Taaffe.

On a bedside table, an assortment of family photos mingles with fresh flowers and jewelry. The unique lamp is made from part of a printing press.

ABOVE: In Fillipa's colorful bedroom, the artwork is by Paul Pack and the lacquered silver bed is from City Joinery.

RIGHT: In Brando's light-filled bedroom at the front of the house, the D. L. desk is by Martin Szekely for Galerie Kreo and the Tizio lamp is from Artemide. The walls are covered with Brandolini fabrics for Holland and Sherry.

A Class Act

MILES REDD'S NEW YORK REGENCY-STYLE TOWNHOUSE

The pretty front façade of the New York townhouse that decorator Miles Redd shares with his sister could double as a Cecil Beaton set for *My Fair Lady*, with its striped blinds and neat Regency-esque front door. Inside, the illusion does not fade: ascending the stairs to the top two floors where Redd has taken up residence, mirrored walls and pale blue silk curtains continue the theatrical flourish.

Although small, the living room, which overlooks the street, is packed with art, furniture, and objects. The parquet floor is intricately detailed into squares, with alternate sections inlaid with chrome strips that are centered with a small chrome square. The cold light of the gray street has been banished here by walls of pink silk and a big red velvet comfortable sofa that takes up almost a third of the available wall space. Wall bracket lamps topped with red shades light the room. Redd's very personal art collection of pastels, drawings, and photographs is carefully arranged around the room. He has also enlivened the space with crystal and glass accents, as well as a large Venetian mirror above the fireplace.

Redd is noted for his sure hand with color, and here he has chosen pale blue to balance the reds of this room. Blue dragonfly cushions are plumped up against the red sofa, and pale blue leather covers the seats of a pair of occasional chairs designed to float around in the room. A well-stocked drinks table in the corner lends a genial feeling of hospitality—a place where friends might meet before a night out on the town.

The adjacent kitchen is a vision of glamour. If Cecil Beaton had ever designed a kitchen, this is what it might look like. With its glossy black cupboards and ceiling, the room nearly disappears, but is brought back to life by the stainless steel appliances and mirrored backsplash, which extends around all three sides. The solid glass countertops are set on an antique mirror and seem to shimmer with the black and silver reflections around the room. To open up the space, Redd painted the floor white; otherwise it might seem too dark. But this is not an ordinary white floor; it is centered by a graphic painted black star, and its boundaries are pinstriped with thin black lines.

Upstairs, the bedroom is a pale blue, and a dramatically oversized canopied bed dominates the room. Made of mirrored glass, it is upholstered in pale blue striped silk. The twin windows are curtained with pale gray silk, to offset the blue walls; the colors of this room are a peaceful silver, white, and black with touches of coral.

But the bedroom is no preparation for the scale of the bathroom next door. Possibly the largest room in the house, it was installed intact as a period mirrored bathroom designed by decorator David Adler and discovered in Chicago. It is a stunningly beautiful space, with a black floor inlaid with chrome in the shape of a decorative cross. The entire wall surface and moldings, except for the bath alcove, are mirrored. Even the built-in dressing table is covered with mirror, and Redd has added a mirrorlike Venetian blind with Grecian-style tapes to match the room's period charm. And as Redd's apartment is small, this room is even used occasionally for dinner parties.

The cheerful living room has pink silk-lined walls. The dark parquet floor has been inlaid with chrome strips in alternating squares. The chimneypiece is packed with personal photographs and enlivened by red pieces of coral, which link this arrangement to the wall color.

This eclectic living room is pulled together by careful use of color; the main piece of furniture here is a red velvet corner sofa lit by red shaded wall lamps. Blue dragonfly cushions lend contrast.

ABOVE: Miles Redd's living room serves many purposes in this diminutive apartment. In this corner, a table functions as a bar, ready to serve drinks to guests, in front of a library stocked with reference books. A bin next to the window provides a place to store rolled up design plans.

RIGHT: Opposite the living room windows, a French Louis XV–style sofa upholstered in white is bounded by two mirrored screens. A large charcoal panther drawing framed in silver hangs on the wall above. The use of glass and mirror in this room makes it appear larger.

ABOVE: The dramatic black kitchen is tempered by a white floor and mirrored countertops and backsplash. Silver and chrome gleam in this sophisticated room. A Miele washer and dryer are set discretely under the counter.

RIGHT: Redd has taken advantage of the high ceilings on the top floor with the scale of this mirrored four-poster bed in the master bedroom. Striped silk accentuates the height of the bed canopy. This restful room is painted a calm blue, accented with curtains of pale gray silk.

FOLLOWING PAGE: This glamorous mirrored bathroom by master decorator David Adler was discovered in Chicago. With very little alterations, it was fitted into this space leading directly from the master bedroom.

Hollywood Regency Revival

KELLY WEARSTLER'S MODERNIST PAVILION IN TROUSDALE ESTATES

Designer Kelly Wearstler's house is a glamorous 1960s Modernist pavilion with Hollywood Regency overtones. Designed by architect Hal Levitt in the Trousdale Estates in Beverly Hills—the spiritual home of Hollywood Regency—here she found the perfect setting for a definitive statement in this eclectic style that she had made her own.

Wearstler's decorating style has evolved dramatically over the last ten years since her first published project, the Avalon Hotel, renovated by Koning Eisenberg Architects, on Olympic Boulevard in Beverly Hills. For the Avalon, she decorated the hotel in harmony with its essentially 1950s architecture. Her style progressed with her dramatic designs for the Viceroy Hotel in Santa Monica to her own revival of Hollywood Regency—a theatrical, mannered style that emerged in Los Angeles in the 1940s and continued to the 1970s. A reaction to the severity of Modernism, Hollywood Regency mixed elements of English Regency with French chic. Popular were mansard roofs and faux pavilions à la Versailles, which borrowed the simple lines of Modernism while adding flourishes taken from eighteenth-century France or Georgian England.

With perfect pitch, Wearstler turned to furnishing her long, low house of white marble and glass using a sophisticated combination of color and pattern. Large perforated screens are a part of her design vocabulary here, giving drama and punch to the main living areas. The house is oriented toward the light, and a high hedge separates it from the street. It has a sense of isolation, with greenery shielding it from other houses, but reveals a striking view across the city to the ocean. The entry area opens up into the main living spaces where long, low sofas keep the room open and airy, and are carefully placed to create several seating areas.

In the "orangerie" wing of the living room, a pair of chairs, two pink corduroy velvet sofas, and a gilt nineteenth-century sofa are anchored by a huge black lacquered coffee table, which is topped by a tray filled with orchids and a large pair of wooden sphinxes. A pair of duchess brisée chairs upholstered in apricot silk is separated by a gilded marble-topped table.

Leading from the living room, the dining room has an entire wall of marble, lit from above by a skylight running the length of the wall. Such a dramatic

RIGHT: In a corner of the living room, a pair of French-style chairs upholstered in apricot silk flank a gilded table topped with marble. A zebra-skin rug covers the floor underneath. The room is given greater depth by the large mirror on the wall behind.

FOLLOWING PAGE: A white marble fireplace extends into a long cool bench in the living room. A live tree shades a seating group, which helps provide a visual separation from the passage to the bedroom.

architectural gesture demands dramatic decorating, and Wearstler has opted for a Chinoiserie style, with Chinese Chippendale-style dining chairs underneath a magnificently bold chandelier. Against the wall she created an arrangement with a striking black armoire flanked by a pair of black pagoda lamps and Rococo mirrors.

Moving on through the house, the den is dominated by a large cast-iron bunch of grapes placed on the coffee table. This room is decorated with acid yellows and accents of red. A large, colorful abstract painting hangs over the yellow sofa, which faces a pair of black Empire-style chairs upholstered in red patent leather that sit against a black and silver Chinese-style screen.

A pair of large green Chinese china dogs guard the entrance to the green library that overlooks the pool at the back of the house. A rock crystal chandelier hangs from the ceiling, catching the outdoor light and adding a note of glamour. This is perhaps where Wearstler has been influenced the most by the great Tony Duquette. The collection of green malachite on the nineteenth-century desk is very much his signature touch, and he would have loved this room.

The main bedroom overlooks the city, and the bed, draped in dark brown linen, is placed to capture the best view of downtown Beverly Hills. It is flanked by a pair of shagrin chests of drawers topped by dramatic bedside lamps made from large pieces of cut crystal. In a corner of the room is a comfortable seating area—a sofa upholstered with a dark brown linen, freshened by white silk cushions, is joined by a pair of armchairs in yellow-green corduroy velvet. From here, the glamorous bathroom in mirror and sliced onyx is a dazzling sight.

Throughout the house, Wearstler uses natural materials as a foil to the sophisticated, grown-up furnishings. The rooms sparkle with rock crystal, quartz, and white coral tablescapes. A petrified tree trunk acts as a coffee table in the den, and a large tree grows indoors next to the fireplace.

The furnishings in the den are a vibrant combination of acid yellows with accents of pink. A bold abstract painting hangs over the gold velvet sofa. An oversized cast-iron bunch of grapes on the coffee table creates scale for the room.

ABOVE: A gilded mirror and chest of drawers topped with a variety of objects made of natural materials seem to glow in a corner of the main living space.

RIGHT: A coromandel screen provides a stunning backdrop to a seating arrangement in one corner of the living room. The low sofa is upholstered in gray-brown velvet.

ABOVE: A zebra-skin rug supplies graphic punch to this small entry area. The mirrored ceiling brightens up the space.

RIGHT: The main dining room features an entire wall of marble lit from above by a skylight running its length. Wearstler has injected the maximum amount of drama in this space with her Chinoiserie-inspired decorating. Yellow Chinese Chippendale–style chairs surrounding the long table provide the dominant color note.

ABOVE: In the master bedroom, four gold-framed abstract artworks surround a faux tortise shell behind the bed, which is draped with dark brown linen.

RIGHT: A wall of onyx provides a glamorous backdrop to a seating arrangement in the master bedroom. Flanking a sofa upholstered in dark brown linen are two armchairs in yellow-green corduroy velvet. The rug under the bed is Imperial Trellis from KWID.

A Prescription for Living

SIMON DOONAN AND JONATHAN ADLER'S NEW YORK APARTMENT

Simon Doonan and Jonathan Adler are one of the most accomplished couples in New York. Doonan, an author and social commentator, is also creative director of Barneys New York, where he has designed their windows on Madison Avenue for many years. These have become more than just clothing displays—they chronicle New York's social life and obsessions and peak every year at Christmas.

Designer and potter Jonathan Adler, his partner of many years, has a chain of stores selling his furniture, rugs, and ceramics that are on the cutting edge of fashionable design. Adler's book, *My Prescription for Anti-Depressive Living*, promotes design as a fun element to brighten up life, rather than a serious business intended to impress.

Both Doonan and Adler have keen radar for popular culture, and their New York City apartment is witness to their many obsessions and enthusiasms. Camp is a theme here, but not content with traditional gay icons, they have gone on a trailblazing path to invent their own iconography.

For example, the upper living room walls arc hung with Pirelli calendars from the 1970s, featuring half-naked girls in artistic poses, while a Mel Ramos print of a model sitting in a bowl of cut fruit appropriately hangs in the chartreuse dining room.

However, their collections are conventionally arranged. Adler collects a little-known genre of kitsch—early-twentieth-century model cars recreated on felt and canvas using found metal objects, mainly watch parts. These pieces are artfully arranged in a small library off the main sitting room, around a wing

chair upholstered traditionally in brown and cream crewelwork fabric. This cozy room is painted dark brown with off-white trim, and stark white pottery made (or collected) by Adler provides fresh accents to liven up the background. A matching pair of white ceramic horses, inspired by Tang statues, has been converted into lamps that are topped with mottled copper-painted paper shades, which give color balance to the room.

Their original apartment has now expanded to include the apartment next door, giving them two double-height living rooms that Adler has used to dramatic advantage. The original room is used by Doonan as an office and workspace, while its twin has walls of brown textured wallpaper, a white fireplace, and two dramatic Suzani panels flanking an impressive suit of armor, which dominates the room. A large horizontal chrome chandelier from the 1960s fills the space, and hovers over an enormous semicircular leather sofa that surrounds a mirrored coffee table. Here, a large Adler flower vase and its contents are reflected in the mirror, around the fireplace. A big brass boot fills the fireplace itself, and on the mirrored hearth rests a bust of the singer Prince, which had been mysteriously decapitated.

Upstairs, Adler adopted a careful palette of red, white, and blue for the master bedroom. The dark

In the entry foyer, a green Chinese console table holds a white ceramic Jonathan Adler lamp, a small whimsical copper statue of Napoleon, and a portrait of their dog, Liberace. The zebras on the floor link the colors of the walls, floor, and rug.

blue walls are uplifted by a white ceiling and trim. A white tallboy picked out in red stands against one wall, while on the other an impressive nineteenth-century Neo-Gothic cheval mirror dominates the rest of the room. The blue-and-white geometric carpet and blue corduroy footstools continue the room's vivid blue undercurrent.

This room has a baronial theme, a reference to a formal and often overlooked European influence on American popular design in the 1960s and 1970s. It was derived from eighteenth-century French furniture and the accoutrements of castles and palaces. When design purists talk about this era, they are usually referring to the elegantly articulated furniture by Knoll or Vladimir Kagan, neglecting the more widespread—and perhaps more inventive—popular design movements here in the United States. Adler has seized upon this as a rich vein of inspiration. The master bathroom includes twin washbasins lit by a pair of black-and-white checked lampshades. Toiletries are hidden by a skirt in the same fabric. The brass shower rod runs around the walls as a kind of picture rail. Above the toilet hangs a large brass "H," a trophy from a Hermès store.

The sunny dining room downstairs is painted a cheerful green and hung with black-and-white printed curtains. Adler chairs surround the dining table that has a permanent display of pottery, usually Adler designs paired with vases from 1960s Denmark, an obvious inspiration for his work.

In the center of the apartment, the two kitchens have been inventively joined together without sacrificing their 1920s charm. Here tea is always made, and home-baked cookies are kept in a refrigerator set into the original dividing wall.

Adler continues the theme of his apartment with his products as a designer and retailer. Here, a recent store interior shows how his life spills over into his design work. The products are part of his furniture line, from the sofa to the X-Benches, and his pottery ranges from vases to lamps and plates. On the mirrored console table, a pair of "bel air" lamps bracket a white-framed mirror. A square white cocktail table displays a selection of Adler vases.

ABOVE: Viewed over the large semicircular leather sofa in the living room, a central mirrored coffee table holds an Adler vase. The inside of the chimneypiece is mirrored as well, which helps brighten the room. Flanking the fireplace, a pair of nineteenth-century-style French chairs display Adler-designed cushions.

RIGHT: In the dining room, painted a cheerful yellow-green, Adler lamps with black shades flank a Mel Ramos print of a model sitting in a bowl of cut fruit, which hangs above a console table. The black lacquer dining chairs are designed by Adler.

ABOVE: Adler collects a little-known genre of early-twentieth-century model cars re-created on felt and canvas using found metal objects, mainly watch parts; here they hang on the dark brown walls of the library. A traditional wing chair upholstered in crewelwork is given a lift by a pillow portrait of their dog, Liberace.

RIGHT: The library has off-white ceiling and trim, and stark white pottery made or collected by Adler provides fresh accents to liven up the dark background. A pair of white ceramic horses, inspired by Tang statues, has been converted into lamps that are topped with mottled copper-painted paper shades, which give the room color balance. The crewelwork fabric on the 1960s chair in the foreground links up with the wing chair in the opposite corner.

ABOVE: A corner of the upstairs master bedroom shows the carefully planned red, white, and blue room. A Union Jack pillow in a white armchair serves to remind Simon Doonan of his British origins.

RIGHT: The bed skirt, curtains, and window blinds are a bright red corduroy, trimmed with decorative red and blue tape. Quirky white pottery figures dangle at the head of the bed. Two Adler X-Benches, upholstered in blue with red trim, rest at the foot of the bed. The cheval mirror reflects the baronial style of the room.

Renovated to Perfection

MATTHEW ROLSTON AND TED RUSSELL'S NEUTRA HOUSE OVERLOOKING LOS ANGELES

Designer Ted Russell knows a masterpiece of modern design when he sees it. Trained in New York, he apprenticed with several renowned decorators before moving to California. He spotted a small advertisement in the *L.A. Times*, and raced up to have a look at this small, beautiful house in Beverly Hills, designed by architect Richard Neutra in the 1960s. His partner, the photographer and director Matthew Rolston, took about a nano-second to agree to buy it, and with very little work, apart from clearing away a few previous additions, they moved into their new house in time for Christmas.

Scattered like small gems in the vast river of Los Angeles's suburban landscape are many of America's most significant mid-century modern houses. Among the most notable are those designed by Richard Neutra, one of the most influential of Modernist residential architects. Born in Vienna, Neutra was lured to the United States in the early 1920s by his friend and fellow Modernist Rudolf Schindler to join him in Frank Lloyd Wright's atelier. Before long both architects had branched out on their own and set up separate offices in Los Angeles, influenced perhaps by the creativity of the Hollywood film industry, but most of all inspired by the freedom to experiment in the warm California climate.

Not long after Russell and Rolston moved in, they had a surprise visitor. The grandson of the original contractor knocked on the door with the house plans, elevations, budgets, and renderings in Neutra's own hand showing how he wanted the interior to look. This gift made them realize that they had a duty to preserve the house as much as possible.

While the front façade provides a stunning view over Los Angeles and the skyscrapers of downtown to the southeast, the house straddles a ridge revealing even greater vistas across the west side of the city, and on a clear day even as far as the island of Catalina on the horizon. Neutra considered this to be the main view, and placed this side of the house in an "L" shape to take advantage of it. Large plate glass windows embrace a pool and terrace, giving most of the rooms a spectacular view. This is not obvious from the entry, however: Neutra designed the house to gradually open up to the drama of the view as the visitor moved through it.

Furnishing the house went smoothly. The couple had lived in modern houses for many years, and already

RIGHT: This characteristic Richard Neutra fireplace in the living room is original to the house. A painting by New York artist Mike Berg hangs on the wall above it. Glimpsed on either side is a pair of Kubos chairs by Josef Hoffmann. In the foreground, a Baccarat one-light candelabra rests on a black wooden Christian Liagre side table.

FOLLOWING PAGES: The exterior of the house glows dramatically in the twilight. Glass walls allow the owners to make the most of Southern California's climate and light. Neutra considered this to be the main exterior, as it looks over a view of the city.

had most of the furniture. Russell carefully placed what they had and worked out where everything should go. When pressed to define their style, Rolston explained, "Our furniture doesn't spring from the mid-twentieth century. My favorite design period is the advent of early Modernism."

The entry leads into the main living room, a sophisticated mix of black-and-white furniture with one bright red armchair providing a powerful accent. Anchored by a black and white Eileen Gray rug, this room looks out past the pool to the view, and to the dining alcove on the left. Russell furnished the latter with bentwood chairs by the early Modernist Josef Hoffmann surround a circular dining table.

Next to the dining alcove, a small comfortable library looks out to the street and the eastern view and is furnished with locally designed furniture. This is their California designers' room—a white sofa by local designer Kerry Joyce sits against the wall behind a coffee table by their good friend Madeline Stuart. Flanking the sofa is a pair of chests of drawers with lamps, all by Charles Fradin. A small wooden stool by Charles Eames acts as a useful occasional table.

To make the most of the view, Russell placed the master bedroom where Neutra had originally planned a small sitting room. This room, almost all glass, is made even more translucent by adding a large mirror above the bed. Transparent Perspex lamps on either side of the bed reflect the room's shimmering light.

High above the bustle of Los Angeles, in perfect tranquility, this mid-century modern house overlooks the view, comfortably distanced from the city that stretches out below like a glittering map.

In the sophisticated black-and-white living room, a bright red upholstered armchair acts as an accent piece. Above the fireplace is a painting by New York artist Mike Berg. The rug is by Eileen Gray, and the larger corner lamp is designed by Fortuny.

ABOVE: In a corner of the living room, a gilded Japanese screen provides a backdrop for one of the Kubos leather chairs. A red side table from Kneedler Fauchere provides a splash of color.

RIGHT: Josef Hoffmann chairs surround a round table by designer Joe D'Urso in the dining alcove, which commands a view of the swimming pool. Ted Russell added an African pestle from Blackman Cruz to give the room a textural note. The painting on the wall behind is by James Nares.

Almost all of the
furniture in the
"California" room
was designed in Los
Angeles. The white
library sofa and
the coffee table are
by Kerry Joyce. A
useful wooden stool
by Charles Eames
can be seen in the
foreground. Flanking
the sofa is a pair
of chests of drawers
by Charles Fradin.

LEFT TO RIGHT: Ted Russell placed a desk by Michael Berman with a matching chair by Waldo Fernandez in the corner of the master bedroom.

The sunny master bedroom is made even brighter by a mirror above the bed. A folded Hermès blanket lies across the foot of a Michael Berman bed.

In the master bedroom, a bamboo and rattan chair sits in front of an industrial metal antique railway safe from the turn of the century. The safe was discovered at Blackman Cruz in West Hollywood.

An original limestone transfer French poster of an Elizabeth Taylor movie hangs next to a black Eileen Gray screen in the study.

Understated Style

PAUL FORTUNE'S HOUSE IN LAUREL CANYON

Paul Fortune is a master of understatement. He has spent more than twenty-five years in this charmingly idiosyncratic house in the Hollywood Hills, originally a cottage built in 1928 for actor Stan Laurel and transformed in the 1930s into a larger house by a Hollywood set designer. Fortune has resisted any temptation to clutter or over-renovate. "There's a certain personality to a house," he says, "and if you remodel too much you lose it." The inspiration was Provençal filtered through a rustic Regency prism. The extra rooms, including those added by Fortune, have been seamlessly integrated into the original building. Built into a hillside, the house was on different levels, and this made it easier to add on to it.

Exactly where Fortune has made these alterations is almost impossible to tell. A good clue is the bathroom fireplace—not the usual location for a chimneypiece when the house was built. Nor was the outdoor shower that fills a conveniently private space next to the bedroom chimney. Fortune uses this as his main shower, and can't understand why people don't do this more often in the mild climate of Los Angeles.

Fortune's belief in classic decorating is clear from his designs for the Sunset Tower Hotel in Hollywood, which is more like a chic but unobtrusive men's club than a hotel. His choice of quiet muted colors and comfortable modern furniture creates an oasis from the teeming Sunset Strip outside.

In his own house, which he shares with landscapist Chris Brock, there is the same feeling of ease, with large well-stuffed sofa cushions and deep-seated chairs. It is reached by stone steps that lead past a Fortune-designed guesthouse and pool on the left, and opens directly onto a large double-height living room with a big stone fireplace at one end. Steps lead up to the bedrooms from this central room, and a curved stair rail defines the entry to the floor downstairs that Brock uses as his study.

The most glamorous room is probably the master bathroom, with counters finished in leather. This is the most recent addition to the house, where Fortune added the fireplace next to a low bathtub, which has been placed in front of a big window overlooking the garden. Original to the house is the "Ship" bedroom, which was designed by the previous owner as a cabin, complete with nautical bunks and a porthole.

"My decorating is not like a Julius Shulman photograph," adds Fortune, who is also the West Coast editor of *House & Garden* magazine. "It is not about being historically accurate; I just put things together with restraint."

RIGHT: Paul Fortune created cozy seating in a window alcove next to the staircase, upholstering the cushions in a sturdy beige cotton. Decorative pillows in a vintage fabric add detail.

FOLLOWING PAGES: The main living room features the original ironwork balustrades. This peaceful but dramatic space has been furnished with a mix of mid-century modern pieces, including a sofa that was inspired by the Biedermeier period from Swedish designer Fritz Henningsen.

ABOVE: A brushed aluminum office chair stands in front of a console table that holds a collection of glass from the 1950s and 1960s from Retro. The painting by Los Angeles artist Charles Fine, which hangs on the wall behind, echoes the watery quality of the glass.

RIGHT: A corner of the master bedroom shows the Fortune-designed chimneypiece. Above it hangs a nineteenth-century Dutch charcoal nude. The Fritz Henningsen chair is upholstered in fabric from Scalamandré.

One section of the living room functions as a library. Fortune designed the coffee table, which works well with the mid-century modern furniture around it. The ceiling lamp is vintage Michael Taylor.

ABOVE: A climbing philodendron lends a tropical note to the outdoor shower that is conveniently shielded by the back of the bedroom's chimney. The plumbing fixtures are from Dornbracht.

RIGHT: The master bathroom was seamlessly added to the house by Fortune. The fireplace is faced with antique stone, and both the floor and countertop are waxed leather. The French 1950s painting was discovered at a flea market. The customized console table comes from Blackman Cruz; a mirror above it reflects the garden view opposite the bathtub.

In the Modern Style

FIROOZ ZAHEDI'S 1920S LOS ANGELES APARTMENT

Photographer Firooz Zahedi loves houses and is constantly seduced by places that have been neglected. He loves the creative process of transforming them so much that his career as one of America's best portrait photographers can often take a back seat to the excitement of a new house or apartment.

Born in Tehran to a diplomatic family, Zahedi has lived all around the world, especially in London, where his stylish parents collected antiques. He moved to the United States to work for his cousin, the Iranian ambassador, where he lived in the lavish and glamorous Iranian Embassy in Washington, D.C., decorated by British decorator Michael Szell.

After training as a diplomat, Zahedi moved onto photography with the encouragement of family friend Elizabeth Taylor, and his first assignments were for Andy Warhol's *Interview* magazine. This led him into the glossy world of celebrity and design, where his taste was formed.

Zahedi bought this 1920s Hancock Park apartment in Los Angeles for its fine Spanish Colonial architecture and central Hollywood location. While Los Angeles is full of apartment buildings, the 1920s apartments like this are unusually well-laid-out, with high ceilings and large windows. When renovating a place like this, Zahedi often considers what the architect would do to improve it using all the new products and technologies available today.

Zahedi recognized the apartment's architectural heritage, but the furniture that he had collected over the years was certainly not Spanish, but instead quite modern with a strong 1970s flavor. He approached the renovation of the apartment carefully, needing to pull together several very different styles and periods. Nonetheless, Zahedi enjoys working quickly; he bought the spacious apartment in July 2003 and moved in two months later, with the renovations completed.

He first stained the new oak floors a rich dark ebony and painted all the walls, including the ornate plaster details, white. All the apartment doors were then lacquered a glossy deep black. This gave him a neutral palette that enabled his carefully chosen furniture, art, and photographs to stand out and create their own environment.

Zahedi's carefully considered design strategy gives his apartment a strong sense of style. Prewar apartments in New York were an inspiration, but Zahedi advises to first look for inspiration in books and magazines for people with similar interests.

The art Zahedi has on display reflects his inspirations—which are other photographers such as Richard Avedon, William Claxton, André Kertész, and Baron de Meyer—rather than the famous faces he has photographed (including classic images of Robert de Niro, Meryl Streep, and Barbra Streisand). He also has a collection of personal gifts given to him by Andy Warhol that mark the beginning of his career.

Zahedi collects movie posters because, in addition to his editorial work, he has produced them for a wide range of films. His collection of old "one sheets," as the posters are called in the industry, acts as an inspiration and a reminder that he himself is part of an old Hollywood tradition.

Of course now that Zahedi has finished this apartment, he will be again avoiding assignments to look for a new design project. "I love the challenges put forth by this passion of mine," he explains. "I can't change the world with all its woes but I can try and make it a little more beautiful in my own way."

The combination of furniture and art in this corner of the living room typifies the care Firooz Zahedi takes with color and shape. The Bertoia Diamond chair in its original orange fabric links with the orange triangle in the 1970s silkscreen on the wall. He lacquered the side table in a shiny black.

The predominantly
1970s furniture in
the main living room
blends comfortably
with Zahedi's
Spanish Colonial–
style apartment.
The Arthur Elrod
chrome sofas are
upholstered in a
café-au-lait ultra-
suede. The Isabella
planters in front of
the fireplace are
by Zahedi's nephew,
furniture designer
Reza Feiz. An Andy
Warhol flower print
decorates the wall
above the mantelpiece.

ABOVE: These Hollywood Regency–style dining room chairs are upholstered in black patent leather. Behind them is a black lacquer credenza, above which hangs a photograph from Zahedi's series of flowers.

RIGHT: This graphic black-and-white corner of the master bedroom is lit by an Art Deco floor lamp. Neutral walls showcase part of Zahedi's photography collection, which includes works by Herb Ritts, André Kertész, and Yul Brynner. In the foreground can be seen the graceful curves of a Hoffmann-style conversation chair.

CLOCKWISE FROM TOP LEFT: Zahedi designed the bar in black lacquer with a white marble top. The original Marlene Dietrich poster framed behind it is from 1932.

A Marilyn Monroe print by Warhol overlooks a mid-century love seat upholstered in beige chenille. The unusual lamp is Italian, from the 1950s.

A Nelson lamp hangs over an elegant 1970s black glass-topped dining table. Hollywood Regency dining chairs against the far wall, upholstered in a Tiffany blue leatherette, balance the room.

The master bedroom features a bed designed by Zahedi, upholstered in brown with chrome legs. The painting on the wall above it is by Stu Sutcliffe, a musician who left the Beatles to pursue his work as an artist.

The custom black lacquer kitchen island designed by Zahedi has a travertine marble top. A collection of black-and-white photography continues the room's color scheme; at left is a photo by Gered Mankowitz, and to the right is a portrait by William Claxton.

A 1970s table with a travertine top and chrome base displays Zahedi's collection of antique and modern boxes.

Designing with Light and Glass

VIDAL AND RONNIE SASSOON'S MID-CENTURY MODERN HOUSE IN BEVERLY HILLS

When Ronnie Sassoon started looking for a home for herself and her husband, the iconic hairdresser Vidal Sassoon, it took her eight months to find this fine example of a mid-century Modernism. However, it still needed a lot of work to reveal the architect's original intent.

Los Angeles architect Hal Levitt was not generally known at the time, but his houses are now becoming sought after. He took the basics of Modernism and added dramatic touches that transported his low single-story houses into places of style and imagination.

"It had the greatest bones I had ever seen," remarks Ronnie. "It also had a very strong personality and started speaking to me right away." She brought in architect Larry Totah to add a library and other necessary architectonic details, and over the sixteen years Ronnie and Vidal have lived in the house, she has refined the decorating to a perfect pitch. "A glass house represents the people inside. It says, 'I am open and vulnerable,' but I thought the personality of the glass softened the industrial-age materials of the house by bringing the outside in," she explains. "This gives a greater sense of softness." The warm and tactile carpeting and the rounded shape of the furniture and art tempers the hard edges of the house, which is like two right angles—a classic "U"-shaped Bauhaus design. The Sassoons find this shape comforting and protective at the same time.

The house is set atop a steep drive. The front façade opens directly onto a cobbled entry courtyard, and its transparency is immediately obvious as the stunning view across the city becomes visible through the glass walls that define the house. However, the coup de grace is the enclosed walkway over the swimming pool. This bridge has several important functions: it forms a courtyard outside the main living area, provides a link between the master bedroom and the public spaces of the house, and creates a dramatic dining space, especially with the tall glass windows pulled back. At no point is the view across the city lost.

Ronnie has kept the furniture low and mono-chromatic to retain the light feeling of the house and to keep the view open. "I have tried to furnish it in the period. It was built on the edge of the 1950s and 1960s, but with its own identity. The art ranges around that period as well, with a few exceptions," she says. The most notable is the large outdoor sculpture by the British artist Anish Kapoor, which dates from 1997. Its rounded shape softens the sharp corners of the pool area.

The Sassoons consider the outside to be part of the house, especially when they entertain, as the plate glass windows all slide open, re-creating its space. Ronnie adds, "I never use flowers in the house as they are not part of what is outside. If I want something organic for the table, I walk outside and pick up pinecones, moss, or bamboo to throw down in a very uncontrived way."

In the media room, the comfortable seating group is angled toward the screen. The 1970 Terrazzo sofas are from Swiss furniture designer de Sede.

The glass windows of this passage, which links the master bedroom to the public areas of the house, slide back, blurring the distinction between indoors and out. A sculpture by British artist Anish Kapoor defines the far end of the swimming pool.

PREVIOUS PAGE: Two Jean Prouvé chairs face a sculpture by Alexander Calder on the coffee table in the main living room. The painting behind the sofa is by artist Lucio Fontana.

LEFT: The artwork on the wall above the dining table is by Etienne Hajdu, a Hungarian artist who worked in Paris.

ABOVE: In this corner of the living room by the front door, the relaxed but stylish seating includes another Jean Prouvé chair and a sofa by architect Lurry Totah.

PREVIOUS PAGES: The living room hearth extends to form a base for an unusual wire sculpture by Bertoia.

Laverne Tulip chairs provide modern seating around a small table in the breakfast nook. The distinctive hanging lamp is by Italian designer Achille Castiglione.

LEFT: The master bedroom bed from Capellini is in front of a shelf holding a collection of photographs that runs along the back wall.

ABOVE: In the library, which leads off the master bedroom, two Flying Chairs by Vernor Panton are suspended dramatically from the ceiling.

PART II

How to Achieve Confident, Bold, and Polished Interiors

New Uses of Color

While all the homes in this book are unique, one element that they have in common is color. No one is afraid of color here—these designers use it with confidence and creativity. Color has many attributes; it can be used to change a space in many different ways. It can create separation, dividing different functions in the same room, or establishing the separate function of another part of the house. In the Ballard house, for example, in which almost all the rooms were painted white to emphasize the quality of the original plaster walls, we painted Liv's office a pale brown to distinguish her workspace from the rest of the house. Color can also modernize an old house or warm up a new one, and can bring the outside in by linking the green of the garden to the house interior. Color can progress through a house from a cool entry hall to a warm dining room at the end of a corridor.

There is nothing else that can change a room so quickly and dramatically as color. A drab, airless space can be transformed into a beautiful room with just a quick coat of fresh paint. A dark, windowless box can be radically changed by using a strong color, while a great piece of furniture can be brilliantly highlighted with a clever choice of paint as background. Even the disadvantages of poorly designed architecture can be minimized with color if it is used with confidence. But this kind of color must be carefully chosen: "I like strong color," says designer Paul Fortune, "but not bright color—people can get

bored with it too easily."

Stripes, either hand-painted or wallpapered, can make a small room look taller. They can be combined with patterned fabrics to great effect. There is no end to a creative approach to walls: they can be combed, dragged, stippled, distressed, and given any number of treatments that can also create texture.

Dark colors, even black, can look stunning with the right combination of furniture. They give a room an expensive, decorated look, and are perfect for city apartments where people love to entertain. And what could be cozier than curling up on a sofa in front of a fire in a dark room with glowing walls to read a good book? Everything else in the room should be bright and light, although a few glossy dark colors on chair seats, for example, help to complete the sophisticated dark theme. It takes courage to paint a room dark. With accents of white, especially for the ceiling, furniture, and woodwork, it can create the feeling of incredible comfort and sophistication. It is perfect for a room that is used a lot at night, and can be as dramatic as red in candlelight. For those who prefer to keep brighter or deeper colors as accents, pale browns and beiges are the best choice for walls. These neutrals encompass a wide range of colors. Blue-beige, green-beige, and yellow-beige are good colors for a peaceful day room, and provide a great background for primitive art and sculpture.

Choice of color can reflect function, mood, and personality. Decorator Martyn Lawrence-Bullard notes, "I have some clients who are upbeat and fun and they love yellows and turquoise, while others who are more dramatic, like myself, prefer red, black, and

PREVIOUS PAGE: An artwork titled *Crocodile Bandage XIV* by brothers Joseph and John Dumbacher forms a background for a sleek bench at their home in Pasadena.

white." Finally, when considering options, it is important to remember that every house responds to color differently. As Florence de Dampierre, who has a wonderful sense of color, cautions, "I love color, but you cannot use the same one in different places, you must adapt it to different lights and locations. A color can look wonderful in the South of France but look completely different in the United States."

White on hand-plastered walls is beautiful. For period houses lucky enough to still have the original walls, the texture of old plaster looks wonderful in plain white. Spanish Colonial and early East Coast Colonial houses look great with white walls when combined with rich dark floors. Furniture, sculpture, and art against white walls make a strong statement, especially if the furniture or the art has a striking shape or silhouette. White also makes a good choice for those who prefer a more neutral tone, like Ronnie Sassoon: "I get tired of color very quickly and I also find it too dramatically influences my mood." There are many different shades of white and they can be used together in the same room, and even on the same door, for a wonderfully subtle effect.

Everybody loves blue. It is a universally popular color. Almost any room could be blue, especially by a lake or the ocean. Adding a hint of brown or gray to blue makes it a more sophisticated color, and any number of shades of blue match when white is added for contrast. Pale blue is very peaceful and is a great choice for a smaller room.

Yellow is the happiest color. It is a good choice for a sunny room, especially in kitchens and breakfast rooms that get the morning light. Added to beige, it makes a sophisticated choice for a living room. In a dark room that has no windows or other features, a very bright yellow as a shock of color can compensate for the sense of claustrophobia in a boxlike space. Like red, it can be used inside bookcases as a small flash of color in an otherwise pale room, or as an accent on furniture. Yellows can range from pale egg yolk to rich golds and lush browns; they are great for warming up a space.

Red always enlivens a room. Red walls in an entryway provide a welcome blast of warmth; in a dining room they create a cozy atmosphere. This versatile color can be a great backdrop for books in the library, tempered with white or off-white trim. Different reds can be used together. It is a perfect color for a dark room that is mainly used at night, as it can look magical with the soft glow of table lamps and the flickering of candles. Many colors go with red, but they should be used as accents so they don't compete with such a strong color. Blue-and-white china looks great in a red room.

Green brings the outdoors in. The vivid hues of the landscape outside repeated in the house give it a fresh and inviting feeling. There are also many beautiful pale greens to choose from. "Recently I had to research the best background color for a set of vitrines which were to display a collection of white ivory," explains designer Ted Russell. "I found that green was considered the ideal color. I tried all the gray-greens and blue-greens in different lights, and eventually matched the color exactly to the agave in the garden." Almost every color goes well with green.

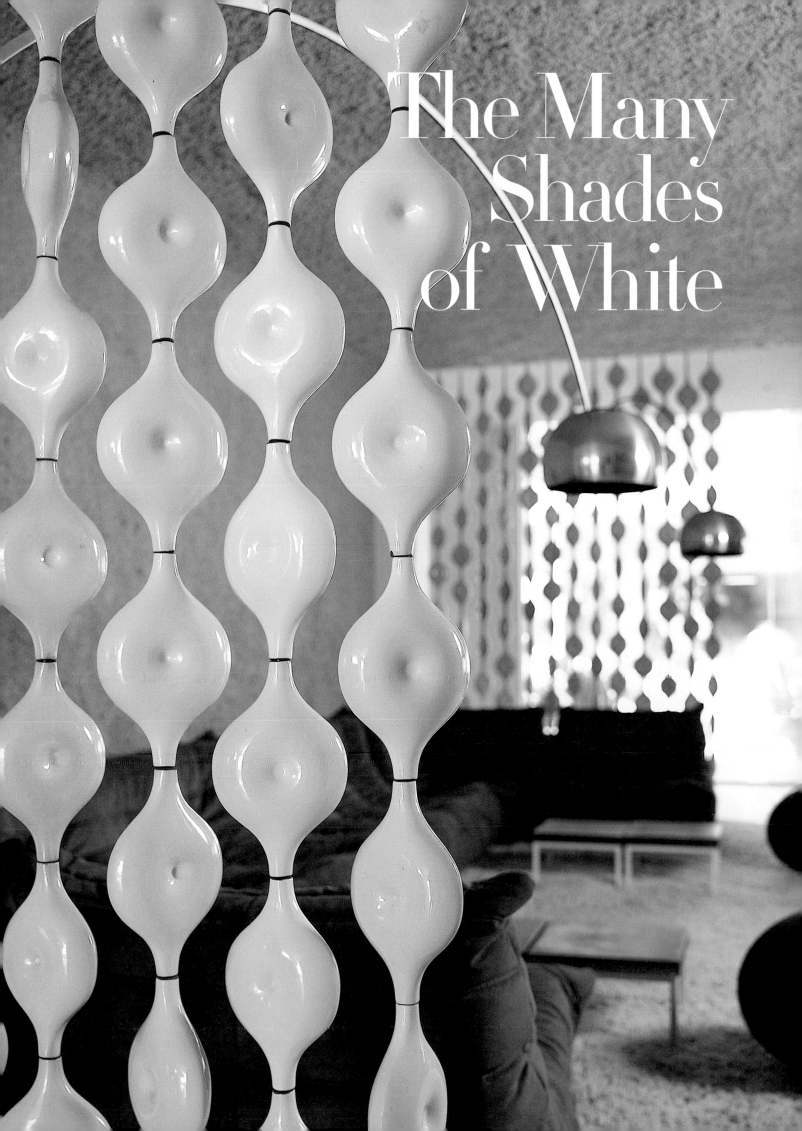

The Many Shades of White

PREVIOUS PAGES: 1stdibs.com founder Michael Bruno's apartment in Paris features objects found on his website. These include the gilded tree at the left, which gives sparkle to a mostly white palette.

The Standard hotel in Los Angeles was designed by Shawn Hausman with a masterful use of materials, such as this white plastic curtain that defines the lobby space.

ABOVE: Decorator Kerry Joyce has a skilled hand with color. Here, he employs a soft palette of whites set off by a graphic black fireplace. An antique glass mirror lends the modern room a feeling of age.

RIGHT: The author designed this recording studio for musician and producer Glen Ballard in whites to give it a soothing, peaceful atmosphere. Hanging star lamps from Maison Midi add to the floating quality of the space.

CLOCKWISE FROM TOP LEFT: Even a simple white room at the beach sometimes needs a note of drama; here, designer Steven Gambrel added just that with a big mounted fish. He used Benjamin Moore paints for this room, as they have a range of subtle whites.

White orchids add a fresh note to an accomplished arrangement by Suzanne Rheinstein.

Michael Trapp in New England is famous for his whimsical store displays. Here, he combines shells, coral, and sculpture to form a harmonious tableau of whites.

Ted Russell put together a monochromatic palette based on white in his entryway. A painting by Stefano hangs above an Andrée Putman console table; it is flanked by a pair of iron andirons in the shape of Egyptian sphinxes. A head of Perseus joins other decorative sculpture and objects on top of the table.

California designer Mark Weaver uses white to show off an unusually shaped chair made with tree roots, and an artwork that seems to float on the wall.

White can be an important backdrop for an interesting collection of furniture. For William Hollaway's French manor house, Jean-Louis Deniot created this elegant and practical arrangement in the entryway.

LEFT: Deborah Berke and Stephen Brockman demonstrate that an all-white room needs to have strong furniture shapes to be interesting.

ABOVE: Nilus de Matran uses translucent panels to continue the ethereal quality of this white bedroom. The only note of contrast comes from a bedside table of light wood.

CLOCKWISE FROM TOP LEFT: Nilus de Matran based the design of this dining room around the painting on the wall behind the white table and black chairs.

Silver is a good choice to liven up an all-white interior. Here, Jean-Louis Deniot adds an assortment of silver and a mirror to this white bathroom.

Michael Bruno added dark touches in this white living room in the Hamptons. A 1940s plaster relief hangs above a mid-century sofa upholstered in its original green leather.

For this corner of a sitting room, Deborah Berke and Stephen Brockman carefully chose the decorative lamp bases to provide contrast in this attractive white space.

Decorator Mark Weaver punctuates this airy white room with bold dark window frames.

Another corner of the Hamptons house decorated by Bruno shows how well white works with a dark wood floor, which he painted with Benjamin Moore paint. The antique clock is lead crystal on bronze.

The
Versatility
of Blue

PREVIOUS PAGES: Benjamin Noriega-Ortiz opted for white as the perfect accent to this strong blue living room.

The Standard hotel in West Hollywood, designed by Shawn Hausman, features many clever uses of color. Here, blue acts as a background for a pair of 1960s hanging chairs.

ABOVE: Tones of blue-gray set off a collection of seashells and coral in this home decorated by Suzanne Rheinstein.

RIGHT: Steven Gambrel designed the cerused ash chair in the entry of his house in Sag Harbor. A pale blue shade from Benjamin Moore opens up the space, which is contrasted with blue-gray accents. The floor is left pale to keep the room fresh.

CLOCKWISE FROM TOP LEFT: Designer Alexandra Champalimaud used a historical blue in her eighteenth-century Colonial house. Most period houses were more colorful than people today realize.

Blue is always a peaceful choice for a bedroom. Here, it is perfectly offset by crisp white bed linens.

In Sag Harbor, New York, decorator Steven Gambrel painted a door a blue-gray to emphasize the period character of his dining room.

A close-up of Gambrel's door shows the richness of the paint quality.

Steven Gambrel painted a series of upstairs rooms in pale shades of blue by Benjamin Moore. Here, the importance of matching the colors in a progression of rooms is demonstrated.

Master decorator John Saladino's apartment in New York inspired many decorators in the 1980s. His distressed wall treatments were innovative and recall his Italian heritage.

ABOVE: Just an accent of blue can enliven dark furniture. Here, decorator Stephen Shadley sets
a blue-gray pot on an Arts and Crafts chest of drawers in the home of actress Diane Keaton.

RIGHT: In the living room of his Paris home, Michael Bruno paired a Cubist painting from
the 1940s with a set of 1940s blue furniture in its original silk that he found on his website
1stdibs.com, which showcases furniture for sale from all over the world.

CLOCKWISE FROM TOP LEFT: Matching the furniture color to the walls can produce a striking effect, as seen here in Laura Dunas's casual outdoor dining area.

Miles Redd creates a sophisticated atmosphere by combining blue with pink and black.

Here, blue makes a good backdrop for a colorful assortment of glasses and other ware in a kitchen designed by architect Benjamin Noriega-Ortiz.

Architectural details enliven the outside of this blue-painted building. Benjamin Noriega-Ortiz used Benjamin Moore paint to create a reflective mood both inside and out.

Blue can make an unexpected combination with purple. With notes of white, this bedroom designed by Waldo Fernandez is both stylish and comfortable.

In a living room, designer Steven Gambrel has added blue touches to the rest of the space to match the walls.

The Diverse Range of Gold

PREVIOUS PAGES: This room by designer Jeff Andrews shows a sophisticated use of browns and golds. The long pot of green plants on the table freshens it up with a contrasting color.

Simon Doonan and Jonathan Adler are enthusiastic collectors of period glass and china, as seen in this display. Adler's finds inspire his own pottery designs.

ABOVE: I decorated this Lloyd Wright studio in a palette of golds, browns, and yellows to create an organic feel to this mainly concrete space. The Moroccan chairs reflect the exoticism of the block pattern Lloyd Wright used to match his father, Frank Lloyd Wright's design for the main house, La Miniatura.

RIGHT: Michael Bruno's Paris apartment is a harmony of browns kept fresh by plaster wall panels and off-white lampshades. Bruno added the Ralph Lauren mohair chairs that rest on a sisal rug as a pale beige contrast to the dark room.

LEFT: Odom Stamps added this dining room to the family house in Pasadena that he shares with his wife, decorator Kate Stamps. The golds and reds make this small room feel cozy. Here they kept the floor pale so as not to overwhelm the space, putting the carpet on the table instead of the floor.

ABOVE: I decorated this Hancock Park living room in lawyer Cathleen Collins's house in pale yellows taken from the rug, which was bought at auction. The colors further lighten up this sunny room; a collection of green pottery adds accent to the shelves at the rear. The furniture is by Barbara Barry for Baker.

ABOVE: Andrew Virtue employs browns and oranges to create a peaceful corner of a living room. A vase of yellow flowers gives life to the vintage Californian pottery arrangement on the beadboard cabinet.

RIGHT: A living room in the Hamptons designed by Steven Gambrel pairs browns and golds in the artwork and furniture with gray window trim. He repeats this cool color in an accent cushion on the brown sofa. All the paint is by Benjamin Moore.

CLOCKWISE FROM TOP LEFT: The main feature of this contemporary room is an orange paintings; the rest of the furnishings have been kept muted. Red pillows on the white sofa add another note of color.

Esprit founder Susie Tompkins chose a pale yellow palette in her San Francisco apartment as a backdrop to her photography collection.

A cool modern dining room in Los Angeles gets a blast of lively orange with Philippe Starck chairs.

A Konstantin Kakanias watercolor was framed in warm wood by decorator Peter Dunham to echo the browns and golds of the tablescape below. A plate by Kakanias joins the eclectic collection of objects.

A careful blend of yellows and golds creates a warm atmosphere in this room by Steven Gambrel.

A log cabin in New Mexico is a natural environment for colors like browns and golds, as in this corner of the late photographer Herb Ritts's bedroom.

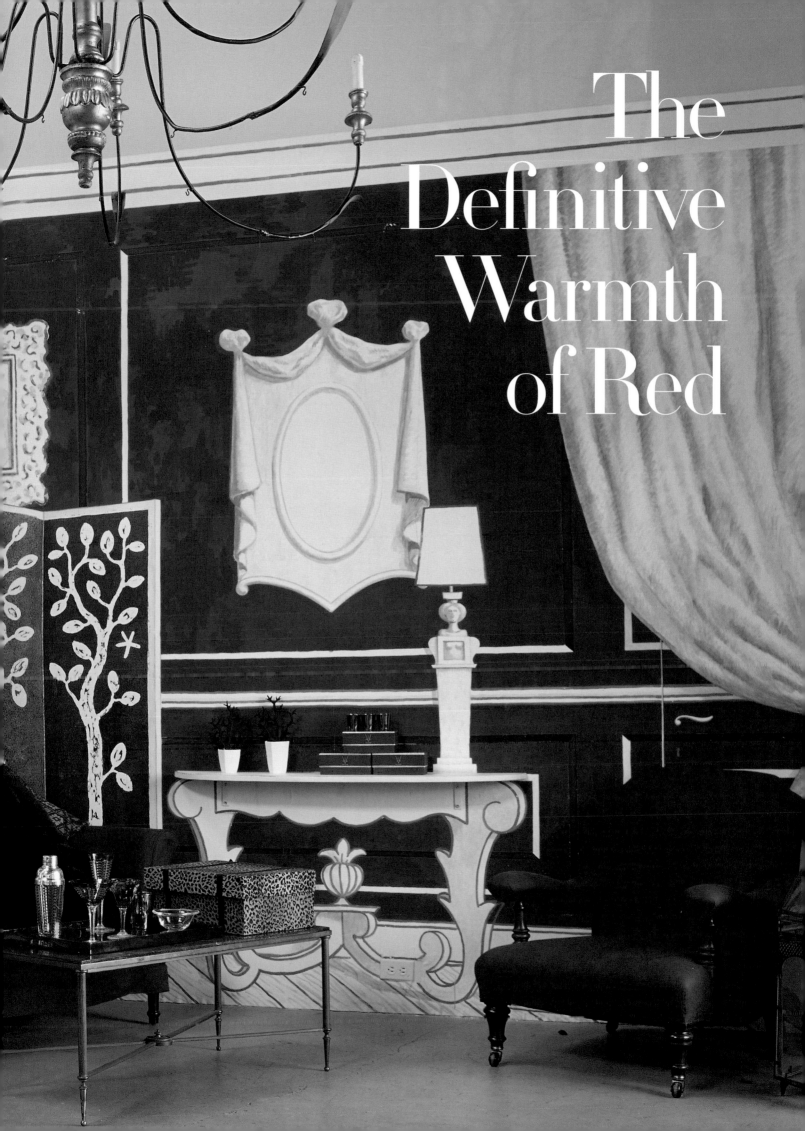

The Definitive Warmth of Red

PREVIOUS PAGE: Designer Suzanne Rheinstein's store Hollyhock is a shopping source for much of the decorating world in Los Angeles. Each Christmas a seasonal red backdrop by French painter Paulin Paris provides a background for Hollyhock's line of chairs.

ABOVE: A New York living room by Miles Redd employs a pink-red as a successful backdrop for a bold black-and-white abstract painting. Redd links this artwork to the room with a zebra-skin chair. This is an unexpected color combination that only an experienced decorator would attempt.

RIGHT: Liv and Glen Ballard's Paris apartment has a cool light, so to warm it up Liv and I added tones of red. We used "Dimity" from Farrow and Ball on the walls and a sophisticated pink for the upholstery and cabinet interior.

LEFT: The Standard hotel in downtown Los Angeles was decorated by Shawn Hausman using vivid color. Here, an arrangement of red sofas is also furnished with long banquettes against the wall, which makes a strong contrast to the black marble floor in the inviting entry lobby.

ABOVE: Los Angeles decorator Jarrett Hedborg uses apple-green furnishings with Benjamin Moore pink walls to create a lively atmosphere for his living room in North Hollywood.

ABOVE: Michael Trapp lives above his garden and antiques shop in the little town of West Cornwall, Connecticut. Skilled in the display of antiques and fabrics, he makes use of reds to create the welcoming haven of a collector and connoisseur. Here, a window seat offers an opportunity to contemplate the garden below.

RIGHT: Trapp also uses reds to unify his wide and varied collections of pottery and furniture. Here, a pile of decorative red trim rests on a carved stone table, waiting for the next decorating project.

CLOCKWISE FROM TOP LEFT: The colors of this red living room are linked together by the nineteenth-century rug. Martyn Lawrence-Bullard added a dark brown coffee table made by his company Martynus-Tripp. The collection of nineteenth-century Imari ware picks up on the reds in this room.

Miles Redd used pink to keep this dark brown entry hall in New York from becoming too somber.

Red is a traditional color for a library. Here at Villa Vallombrosa, I added a large-scale Thai temple vessel to the table to match the red walls and curtains. Bamboo furniture adds to the Chinoiserie style of the room, and a sisal mat on the floor keeps the room from becoming too dark.

Decorator Tom Beeton uses a sophisticated pink in this formal dining room. This color creates a flattering reflection on people's faces while they are dining, which is especially effective when lit with candles.

Martyn Lawrence-Bullard hung a round nineteenth-century mirror over the seventeenth-century Flemish tapestry in this rich living room in West Hollywood. This nineteenth-century French club sofa is upholstered with brown silk-velvet, and the touches of red in the surrounding chairs and cushions create a luxurious effect.

Our eighteenth-century farmhouse in Connecticut is painted a traditional red. I added white wicker chairs and tin wall plates to give the front porch more definition.

The
Freshness
of Green

PREVIOUS PAGES: The pale green living room of Kate and Odom Stamps's home in Pasadena is a perfect setting to showcase their collection of eighteenth- and nineteenth-century watercolors.

This Richard Neutra house has its original bathroom, which has been painted a period green.

CLOCKWISE FROM TOP LEFT: Alexandra Champalimaud used soft, historically inspired gray-greens upstairs in her Litchfield, Connecticut, house to give the stairwell a peaceful quality.

Notes of bright green freshen up a bedroom in my eighteenth-century Connecticut farmhouse, reflecting the color of the surrounding countryside. The crewelwork on the bed canopy has touches of the same color. A black shawl at the end of the bed provides contrast.

Stephen Shadley arranged his client's green pottery collection in this small corner cupboard with red interior walls to create a color accent for the room.

A small orderly table arrangement by Suzanne Rheinstein sits in this guest bedroom.

Jean-Louis Deniot incorporates just a few pieces of green glass to match the color of the sink skirt in this tiny Parisian apartment kitchen. A stainless steel sink and matching objects combine with white to provide background color.

The green walls of this kitchen are a backdrop to a collection of framed pressed plants in William Hollaway's kitchen in Chantilly, France, designed by decorator Jean-Louis Deniot.

The green theme of Sean
Mathis and Florence de
Dampierre's library in
Litchfield, Connecticut, is
accented with orange.
A French eighteenth-century
child's chair has been
upholstered in this vivid
color to tie in with the
pillows on the sofa
opposite. De Dampierre
even added a line of
orange next to the ceiling
moldings. The gold-framed
mirror is late-eighteenth-
century American.

CLOCKWISE FROM TOP LEFT: The crisp modern lines of the furniture are showcased in this bedroom by architect Benjamin Noriega-Ortiz.

Here, Noriega-Ortiz used an artwork to bring a green accent into this stylish modern room.

Green is a traditional color for awnings. In this Victorian house owned by Jock and Alexandra Spivy, they shade a table set for lunch.

The bath towels match the color of the laundry here in a room designed by Nate Berkus.

Kelly Wearstler used green as the main color accent in this bedroom. The chrome bed provides a slick modern touch and adds to the room's geometric feel.

Plants add to the natural effect of texture on this green wall.

Comfort and Rest

INNOVATIVE DESIGNS FOR THE BEDROOM

Your bedroom is a wonderful opportunity to create a dreamlike fantasy space. Here, personal expression can be hidden from the more public living rooms. However, whatever your choice, Ronnie Sassoon notes that it is important to keep the room "peacefully and decoratively quiet."

One of the most important principles in decorating a bedroom is to make it comfortable—this is the ultimate luxury. With so many design choices today, it is easy for designers to make a bedroom as beautiful or as minimal as possible without sacrificing comfort. "We have too much of a tendency to admire rooms in photographs," advises decorator and author Florence de Dampierre, "but it is very important to understand what you expect from a room. The first rule of every house is that it should be comfortable before it looks good."

The bed is the centerpiece of the room and is where we spend more time than anywhere else. We sleep, relax, read, watch television, and sometimes even eat in our beds. Beds come in all shapes and sizes. The four-poster is a popular choice. It reminds us of our ancestors, when bedrooms needed an extra chamber for warmth, and the sense of enclosure that they offer still creates a feeling of restful security. A four-poster also adds a sense of drama to the room, whether it is a simple steel frame or ornate with frills, curtains, and fringing. Headboards personalize a bed, and they can be in many colors and materials. The most economical and comfortable choice that goes with any room is a padded headboard. This can be covered with any color or patterned fabric to harmonize with the rest of the bedroom. Beds can be decorated with many cushions and pillows and are often used to display a textile collection. Layers of carefully composed ornamental and functional pillows can create an exotic environment.

Having chosen the bed, the next decision is what to put next to it. Bedside tables, those convenient places for bedtime essentials, need to be a practical size: large enough for a good book, a carafe of water, and a strong reading light. They add a decorative flourish to the room and come in endless variations ranging from serious antique tables to benches, plastic cubes, or Moroccan chairs. A bedside table also helps with scale. A bed can be a very large object for a not too large space. The bedside tables, which are like little satellites, help scale down the size of the bed. The rest of the bedroom furnishings may be kept quite simple. A soft rug or carpet on the floor provides comfort on a cold morning. A well-upholstered armchair and footstool offers a good place to read a book without actually going to bed.

The right paint colors are important, too. Dark colors give a feeling of enclosure, while pale colors create an atmosphere of peace and tranquility. The only colors to avoid are the brighter shades, which can be too harsh in the morning light.

Comfort is also about good lighting, and in the bedroom that means soft lighting, not drugstore-bright lights. Dimmers are perfect, but better still are the soft pools of light thrown by table lamps. Resist installing recessed lights that lend the ceiling an institutional look: a beautiful room can be ruined by a glance upward to reveal a forest of cans and grills in the ceiling. Even speaker systems can be hidden, recessed invisibly into the plaster or painted to look like the wall. Antique chandeliers can make a room dazzle, and wonderful modern versions often work well in a contemporary-style house.

The bedrooms illustrated on the pages that follow have been chosen because they have very personal and different elements in their design.

This comfortable bedroom with plenty of pillows was designed by decorator Tom Beeton for a client in Santa Barbara. The silk bedcover and canopy create a feeling of luxury.

Designer Lynn von Kersting shows her skill in creating a comfortable bedroom using many different fabric patterns. Down-filled cushions add to the sense of sumptuousness of the sofa and armchairs in the seating arrangement at the foot of the draped four-poster bed. Much of the furniture comes from von Kersting's store Indigo Seas in Los Angeles.

CLOCKWISE FROM TOP LEFT: A Ralph Lauren bed is made up with custom sheets from Prima Linea in the Paris apartment of Michael Bruno. A vintage embossed leather chest of drawers acts as a nightstand.

Martyn Lawrence-Bullard designed this bedroom in Los Angeles with a bed from Martynus-Tripp, using antique furniture and mirrors. The curtains, cushions, bedspread, and Venetian gondola chair are all covered with many different antique paisley fabrics.

Fritz and Dana Rohn draped their four-poster bed with antique textiles to create a more intimate space. The painted chest came from Jennings and Rohn, their antiques store in Woodbury, Connecticut.

This dark bedroom designed by Nate Berkus inspires restful sleep. The headboard is upholstered in brown leather.

Custom silk-velvet pillows from Alan Dougal mix with antique Fortuny fabric pillows to make this Colonial-style bed very comfortable. Martyn Lawrence-Bullard decorated the walls with early engravings of Shakespearean scenes.

ABOVE: Kate Stamps designed this bedroom for her daughter, Emma. The freestanding dressed four-poster bed is the main feature of the hexagon-shaped room. It is a useful daybed as well.

RIGHT: An antique dressmaker's dummy is an eclectic touch in this Barbara Barry bedroom.

CLOCKWISE FROM TOP LEFT: The bolster that I added to Michael Besman's bedroom provides extra comfort and a design accent to the bed. An antique Chinese chest serves as a bedside table.

Martyn Lawrence-Bullard hung a seventeenth-century Coromandel screen above this bed in New Mexico. He created matching lamps with nineteenth-century Chinese wine jars. The Pratesi sheets on the bed are topped with a nineteenth-century paisley throw.

I created a bedroom in this small attic in Paris using a nineteenth-century pullout bed found in Los Angeles. Creating a tentlike atmosphere made the small space feel larger. The fabric is from Chelsea Textiles.

This cozy country bedroom has the warmth of natural materials. A Hermès blanket lies across the bed.

In Cathleen Collins's Hancock Park house, the bedside tables are designed by Kerry Joyce, and the bedside lamps are from Vaughan. I added extra pillows for late-night TV viewing.

A balanced collection of cushions makes this bed comfortable. The bed linen borders echo the frame of the architectural print hanging on the wall above. The tiger-skin pillows and plain upholstered headboard give the room a masculine feel.

LEFT: Collections of books and framed photographs give an atelier look to this bedroom with a perfectly scaled, patinaed Chinese red lacquer cabinet, which helps store unnecessary clutter. The peaceful color of this room, designed by Waldo Fernandez, makes it a restful place to sleep.

ABOVE: This spacious bedroom, designed by Kelly Harmon, is given architectural character with shuttered octagonal windows and exposed roof trusses. An antique box at the end of the bed provides storage.

CLOCKWISE FROM TOP LEFT: This modern bedroom has a
headboard which incorporates two bedside tables.
A second padded headboard provides extra support.

Architect Brian Murphy likes to use natural materials. Here,
tree logs function as bedside tables. A bamboo screen adds
texture to the room.

The New York bedroom of artists Joseph and John Dumbacher is
a working space that opens up to two beds on either side. This
is a clever way to make the most of limited space.

A strong abstract painting can be a good starting point for
decorating a room. Here, a modern blond wood bed has
an extra sheepskin throw for warmth.

This bedroom has plenty of light and feels like sleeping in
a tree house. Brian Murphy designed a circular window that
has a treetop view.

New Solutions

MODERN DESIGNS FOR THE KITCHEN AND BATHROOM

America now lives in the kitchen. It is the most popular room in the house, where renovating can add the most value. Busy families gather in the kitchen, which in recent years has evolved into an extended space in which people eat, sit, read, watch television, and do homework. This has led to the evolution of a huge industry that deals with the needs of this space. In addition to decorators, kitchen designers, media consultants, and lighting specialists all have a hand in the modern kitchen. Today's kitchens should be planned to look like the rest of the house, as a contemporary-style kitchen can look alien in a nineteenth-century townhouse, while a traditional kitchen in a modern house looks fussy. However large the overall space is, the working area itself should not be too big. A cook needs to move from countertop to sink to stove easily, without having to cross a large room. "A galley kitchen works perfectly well," advises Ronnie Sassoon, who often entertains large groups of friends. Lots of countertop surface is important, as is plenty of room for storage space, and an old-fashioned pantry is a great extension to the kitchen. Today, most cabinets reach to the ceiling to provide extra storage space. Finally, every kitchen needs at least two sinks so that more than one person can be using one at the same time. Some people even like to have two dishwashers for big families or large parties.

The simplest kitchen surfaces should be chosen as a backdrop, usually plain tiles and floorings which can then be personalized with splashes of color inside glass-fronted cabinets or with a dramatic light fitting. Designing a kitchen too creatively—with hard-to-replace vividly patterned tile, for example—may also make it hard for someone else to live there one day. "I have always loved mirrored back-splashes," says decorator Ted Russell, "especially for a smaller kitchen. It gives the room a lot of glamour." Appropriate lighting is as important in the kitchen as it is in the bedroom. The most discreet—and practical—is under-cabinet lighting, with spotlights over the sink and stove. While a good designer provides plenty of outlets for appliances, a dramatic chandelier in the style of the kitchen can provide just the right finishing touch.

For additional space, sometimes it is more economical and visually interesting to add furniture such as freestanding cupboards or butcher-block center tables. These can be antique or stainless steel, depending on the style of the kitchen.

There are thousands of flooring choices for kitchens. While tile and stone floors may look beautiful, they can be hard to stand on after a few hours, and many people prefer wood or linoleum. There is nothing more pleasant than a good-looking wooden kitchen floor. Countertop materials are another important kitchen decision. These materials also go in and out of fashion. Granite can look dated, cleaning grouted tile can be a chore; wood needs constant maintenance, while marble can stain. One of the most popular choices today is sandstone, because it is easy to maintain.

Decorate your kitchen as though it is the living room; there is little point in having the best art and furniture in another room which is rarely used. And, what could be more attractive than cooking in a room surrounded by your favorite things?

This Spanish Colonial–style kitchen in Liv and Glen Ballard's house had none of its original cabinetry when I started to work on it. We kept the shell of the new cabinets, but the doors were all upgraded. The plaster ceiling was studded with large can lights, which were removed and replaced with one graceful light in the center and task lighting under the cupboards.

LEFT: Muriel Brandolini designed this kitchen in the basement of her Manhattan townhouse. The ceiling fixture is a Zettel'z 5 from Ingo Maurer, and the 1940s marble table is by Jean Dunand. The zinc cabinetry is from Cicognani. Thonet bentwood chairs surround the table.

ABOVE: This attractive white kitchen designed by Heather Chadduk blends in with the style of the rest of the house. The blackboard above the period stove is a wonderful idea for a busy cook.

CLOCKWISE FROM TOP LEFT: Michael Anderson redid the kitchen in his Spanish Colonial–style house to have more of a Mexican atmosphere: he painted it a bright yellow and upgraded the floor with terracotta tiles.

Miles Redd designed this sophisticated New York kitchen with black cabinets. White marble countertops and stainless steel appliances give balance to the dark room.

Open shelving can be a design statement in the kitchen. Here is a charming display of china, fruit, flowers, and other objects.

Architect Scott Johnson designed this bold modern kitchen for a house he built in Los Angeles—a good example of matching the room to the architecture.

An extra kitchen sink is always useful for a companion cook.

This beautiful sink in Alexandra Champalimaud's Colonial kitchen shows the quality of vintage pieces. Red stools provide a colorful accent to the room.

LEFT: This well-planned kitchen in the Hollywood Hills was designed by Smith Miller Hawkins. It offers plenty of light and working space.

ABOVE: This kitchen by Roy McMakin shows a typical work triangle between sink, stove, and refrigerator. Its neutral style would suit most houses.

CLOCKWISE FROM TOP LEFT: Decorator Kelly Harmon installed a large stove with a correspondingly large hood in her French-style kitchen.

A vintage refrigerator can be the focal point of the kitchen and gives period charm to a modern space.

Plenty of space in the kitchen gave designer Suzanne Rheinstein a chance to include an antique-style table in the center. Large windows make the most of garden views.

Open shelves offer an easy way to quickly find plates in this kitchen designed by Barbara Barry. The all-white china and painted cupboards become a backdrop for the room.

Steven Shadley successfully incorporated a modern kitchen in this traditional Spanish Colonial–style home in Beverly Hills. The stainless steel countertops and appliances create unity, and the overscaled light fitting adds drama to the room.

Brunswich et Fils library wallpaper transforms this small kitchen designed by Martyn Lawrence-Bullard. A Martynus-Tripp butcher-block table in the center of the room adds extra workspace.

t

The Virginia decorator Nancy Lancaster believed in decorating the bathroom as though it was a living room, with painted walls, artwork, and window blinds, and furniture chosen for comfort as well as looks. The style caught on in the 1930s, and Americans have been decorating their bathrooms ever since. Modern bathrooms have also been greatly influenced by resort hotel design, where guests have more time to slow down and discover what a pleasure it is to have a well-designed bathroom. Once back home they search for the same amenities and even perhaps a sense of resort fantasy, such as a beautiful view, lots of space and mirrors, or a freestanding bathtub that gives an instant feeling of a resort.

Like kitchens, the simplest design is best for bathrooms, and they should look like they belong to the overall style of the house. Bold colors are usually avoided, as today these rooms are often designed with a spalike atmosphere in mind. The most expensive elements of a bathroom—the tiles, fixtures, and fittings—are usually as plain as possible, to act as a backdrop for more personal design statements. Decorator Muriel Brandolini, for example, kept her bathroom faucets and sinks plain and unadorned but hung the walls with her own fabrics, creating a fantasy chamber.

Many bathrooms today are larger than they were in the past, with twin sinks, plenty of space for towels, and the toilct shielded by a discrete wall. For a well-finished look, showers are usually tiled up to the ceiling, and if well planned, may not need a shower curtain, nor an intrusive glass door or cubicle. Bathtubs centrally placed in the middle of the room have a theatrical quality, transforming a daily task with a dramatic flourish.

Here, designer Kerry Joyce has created a beautiful bathroom with simplicity as its main feature; its spare look includes a freestanding bathtub next to a tall framed mirror and large attractive windows that overlook the garden.

ABOVE: For this stylish modern bathroom, Moses Becker added a wooden chair to lend an organic touch that tempers the severity of the room.

RIGHT: Many designers choose to ignore the period style of the house when they are designing a bathroom. Here, Karin Blake incorporates a bathroom without losing the character of the original architecture.

CLOCKWISE FROM TOP LEFT: An antique French corner washstand still serves a purpose in this bathroom by New York decorator Jean-Louis Deniot.

To expand film producer Michael Besman's master bathroom, I took out a bedroom shelving alcove on the other side of the wall. The stainless steel cabinet is from Liz's Antique Hardware, a popular store in Los Angeles for restorers.

This spalike bathroom was designed by Kelly Harmon to provide a garden view from the tub. A crystal chandelier adds a touch of sparkle.

Bathrooms can be added to old houses without changing the exterior. Jean-Louis Deniot fitted this one into a small space next to a guest bedroom. A gilded framed mirror picked up at a flea market makes an economical choice for the wall above the sink.

Jock and Alexandra Spivy restored their nineteenth-century house in New York State, adding this new bathroom in the style of the house; today the plumbing fixtures needed to create a period bathroom are readily available.

Even all-white bathrooms can be full of character. Heather Chadduk designed this charming room in California.

LEFT TO RIGHT: Architect Mark Mack designed this colorful bathroom with abstract panels of color, which extend to the tile as well as the cabinets. The walls were kept pale to provide balance.

Simon Doonan and Jonathon Adler's enthusiasms for clothing and pottery spill over into the bathroom design in their New York apartment. An abstract artwork on the wall adds even more color.

This elegant bathroom, with its clever use of shape and color, was designed by architect Josh Schweitzer for the actress Diane Keaton.

CLOCKWISE FROM TOP LEFT: The entry to Barbara Barry's original 1930s bathroom in Los Angeles is furnished with an Art Deco console table.

This masculine bathroom has a beautifully crafted antique cupboard, which houses the sink.

Martyn Lawrence-Bullard gave this bathroom an exotic feel, with plaster walls edged with Moroccan tile. He used a Turkish ticking fabric from Martynus-Tripp for the shower curtains. A couple of Syrian stools give it the finishing touch.

This small bathroom was transformed with luxurious details, including a marble-topped sink custom-made for Lawrence-Bullard by the firm Martynus-Tripp. A nineteenth-century bamboo shade covers the window next to a mirror from Waterworks.

Michael Trapp created a fantasy bathroom for himself at his home in Connecticut, with a metal bathtub set next to a casually draped window. Rows of red trim run along the top of this cozy alcove.

Monogrammed Ralph Lauren towels hang in this Victorian-inspired bathroom by Lawrence-Bullard. Gold-topped Asprey bottles decorate a nineteenth-century bamboo shaving stand.

Outdoor Spaces

STYLISH DECORATING IDEAS FOR ENTERTAINING

Americans have always entertained in style. After their first harvest, the pilgrims' feast of 1621 went on for three days and included ninety Native Americans with huge amounts of food either grown in the fields or hunted from the surrounding forests. By the nineteenth century, dining had evolved into a complicated and ritualized affair, with hundreds of utensils and accoutrements and carefully devised rules for their use; the formal meal became a theatrical performance. Today, while traces of this are still visible at gala events and political and diplomatic dinners at the White House, for the most part the American tradition of entertaining has become more casual. This relaxed approach has led to including the garden in the search for available space. Decorator Florence de Dampierre built her pool house with that specifically in mind, with plenty of patios and outdoor seating areas where she can easily accommodate more people.

In warm weather, every space in the garden can be used for dining: tables and chairs can be moved to take advantage of a view, or a little-used corner can be turned into a charming outdoor dining room. Decorator Kate Stamps took the space between the back of an apartment and the side wall of the garage and transformed it into one of the nicest parts of the house with the help of a few potted plants, a trellis, and some outdoor tiles set in sand without grout. There is often more space in the garden than inside, and California landscape designer Nancy Power added a fireplace at the back of her house so she can entertain all year round, with a table and chairs set outdoors in front of a roaring winter fire.

Both indoors and outdoors, design is an important part of creating an inviting atmosphere. Today, thanks to the global marketplace, there are thousands of colorful and delightful accessories for the table, and every season brings a different style or theme as an occasion for meals and parties. Stores like Pottery Barn and Crate & Barrel carry bright and cheerful plates and linens that change every few months according to the time of year. "I love to set the table the afternoon before a dinner party," says Ted Russell. "That way you can try out different centerpieces during the day. It's like buying Christmas presents months before Christmas!" he exclaims.

Ronnie Sassoon and her husband Vidal entertain frequently and with great creativity in their mid-century modern house in Beverly Hills. Her advice is to "keep it simple," which is a style that suits their minimalist aesthetic.

As with the Sassoons, setting a table can become a sculptural affair, using natural materials and elegant shapes. Even the colors of the food can complement the bowls and plates as the meal progresses. It is important to make sure that guests are comfortable. "You have to have a place for people to sit," reminds Marian McEvoy, whose advice on entertaining can be found in a monthly column for *Domino* magazine. Her verandah overlooking the Hudson River is cleverly planned for summer entertaining—the black wicker chairs are deliberately small in scale to fit the maximum number of friends. The colors are fresh blue and white, and she carries this theme along the verandah's forty-foot length. One of the things in common with all the decorators in this book is that they love entertaining. "My own house has a magic that puts people at ease," explains designer and magazine editor Paul Fortune, "there's a roaring fire, flowers, and the lighting is attractive. If you create a spell, it can become magic. It's about all the little elements." However, de Dampierre notes, "The most important part of entertaining is to have fun yourself."

Decorator Kate Stamps created a shady outdoor dining room at the rear of a Los Angeles apartment by constructing an arbor covered with flowering creepers.

Decorator Rose Tarlow set a couple of chairs outside next to the flowering wisteria for afternoon tea. Almost anywhere in the garden can be a great place to entertain, even if just for two.

ABOVE: This Spanish Colonial—style courtyard has been transformed into a Moroccan outdoor living room by Martyn Lawrence-Bullard, who combines lamps, an exotic mirror, and a nineteenth-century brass-topped wooden Indian table to evoke a Middle Eastern atmosphere. A pillow-laden English antique crib is an inviting outdoor sofa.

RIGHT: With such a display of vivid bougainvillea on this terrace at the back of a client's house, decorator Nate Berkus naturally chose pink for the outdoor cushions and tablecloth.

CLOCKWISE FROM TOP LEFT: An assorted collection of vintage Moroccan lanterns hangs from a tree trunk that has been integrated into this patio. When he lived here, Martyn Lawrence-Bullard decorated this space as though it were indoors, bringing out antique Fortuny pillows and furniture whenever he needed to entertain.

Here, Lawrence-Bullard stenciled the walls of an outdoor arbor to match exterior tiles in the garden. The mirrored niche reflects Moorish-style lanterns.

Jeff Andrews used these striking blue wicker chairs as the focal point for this dining area. Spanish–style lamps over the table add more atmosphere.

The scent of lemons perfumes this outdoor living room. A sofa piled high with Indian fabric cushions provides a cool seat underneath the tree.

Liv Ballard found these votive candleholders at Indigo Seas— a match for the original tile on her outdoor fountain. At night, when the candles are lit, they illuminate the tile's beauty.

This courtyard in designer Tom Callaway's house is decorated for a Spanish Colonial–style Christmas party.

ABOVE: Decorator Tom Beeton made the most of this small terrace at the back of his house in West Hollywood. Shaded by a pair of eucalyptus, a stone table sits in the center of the space. A birdcage filled with candles provides the lighting. Other furniture is brought out when needed.

RIGHT: Landscape designer Rob Steiner created this gazebo to enlarge the space of the house. Translucent fabric suspended over this Asian-style dining table offers shade for guests.

LEFT: An outdoor living and dining space set for dinner is defined by a canvas awning that matches the striped director's chairs around the table. An outdoor fireplace warms a living space behind the dining area.

ABOVE: This graceful Pasadena garden belonging to Jim Watterson and George Martin is at its best when the white wisteria flowers. Cane chairs surround a table set for drinks in the afternoon sun.

CLOCKWISE FROM TOP LEFT: Florence de Dampierre sets these rustic table and chairs outside for iced coffee in the afternoon at the rear of her eighteenth-century house in Litchfield, Connecticut.

An elegant modern dining table is laid with style and simplicity; Ronnie Sassoon cut palm fronds from her garden to act as place mats.

Another view of the outdoor living and dining area on page 250, shown here without the table; the space becomes a separate room during the day.

Ted Russell laid this table for dinner outside the Neutra house he shares with photographer Matthew Rolston. A Baccarat one-light candelabra is the centerpiece for this modern setting.

In this beachside backyard, the color of the sea is echoed in the blue glasses set on the table and in the hammock pillow beyond.

Design Directory

The following is a list of many of the interior designers and decorators who are featured in this book. Several have their own furnishing lines and shops.

Alexandra Champalimaud
Alexandra Champalimaud &
Associates
One Union Square West,
Suite 705
New York, New York 10003
www.alexchamp.com
Nataliew@alexchamp.com

Barbara Barry
Barbara Barry, Inc.
9526 Pico Boulevard
Los Angeles, California 90035
310-276-9977
www.BarbaraBarry.com

Tom Beeton
tombeeton@msn.com

Muriel Brandolini
525 East 72nd Street
New York, New York 10021
212-249-4920
www.murielbrandolini.com

Michael Bruno
646-435-8956
micahelbruno@1stdibs.com
www.1stdibs.com

Thomas Callaway
2920 Nebraska Avenue
Santa Monica, California 90404
310-828-1030

Florence de Dampierre
P.O. Box 1576
Litchfield, Connecticut 06759
Fdedampierre@aol.com

Deborah Berke and Stephen
Brockman
Deborah Berke & Partners
Architects LLP
220 Fifth Avenue
New York, New York 10001
212-229-9211
www.dberke.com

Jean-Louis Deniot
Jean-Louis Deniot Inc.
12 East 86th Street
New York, New York 10028
917-705-1318
www.deniot.com

Paul Fortune
1809 Jewett Drive
Los Angeles, California 90046
Mail@paulfortune.com

Steven Gambrel
S. R. Gambrel Inc.
270 Lafayette Street, Suite 805
New York, New York 10012
212-925-3380
www.srgambrel.com

Kelly Harmon
6261 Ebbtide Way
Malibu, California 90265

Suzanne Rheinstein
Hollyhock
817 Hilldale Avenue
West Hollywood, California
90069
310-777-0100
www.hollyhockinc.com

Lynn von Kearsting
Indigo Seas
123 North Robertson Boulevard
Los Angeles, California 90048
310-550-8758

Jarrett Hedborg
Jarrett Hedborg Interior Design
8811 Alden Drive, Suite 11
Los Angeles, California 90048
310-271-1437

Jeff Andrews
Jeff Andrews - Design
354 West Avenue 42
Los Angeles, California 90065
323-227-9777
www.jeffandrews-design.com

Jonathan Adler
Jonathan Adler Interior Design
212-645-2802
www.jonathanadler.com
For interior design projects,
contact id@jonathanadler.com

Scott Johnson
Johnson Fain
1201 North Broadway
Los Angeles, California 90012
323-224-6000
www.johnsonfain.com

Kelly Wearstler
KWID
317 North Kings Road
West Hollywood, California
90048
323-951-7454
www.kwid.com

Karin Blake
Karin Blake Designs
49 A Malibu Colony
Malibu, California 90265
310-456-8010

Kerry Joyce
Kerry Joyce Associates Inc.
115 North La Brea Avenue
Los Angeles, California 90036
323-938-4442
www.kerryjoyce,com

Mark Weaver
Mark Weaver & Associates, Inc.
519 North La Cienega Boulevard,
Suite 11
West Hollywood, California
90048
310-855-0400
www.markweaver.com

Martyn Lawrence-Bullard
Martyn Lawrence-Bullard
Designs
323-512-2959

Roy McMakin
McMakin Studio
1422 34th Avenue
Seattle, Washington 98122
206-323-0198
www.domesticfurniture.com

Michael Trapp
Michael Trapp, Inc.
7 River Road
West Cornwall, Connecticut
06796
860-672-6098
www.michaeltrapp.com

Nate Berkus
Nate Berkus Associates
311 West Superior Street,
Suite 110
Chicago, Illinois 60610
312-492-0660
www.nateberkus.com

Nilus de Matran
Nilus Designs
757A Pennsylvania
San Francisco, California 94107
415-826-3434
www.nilusdesigns.com

Benjamin Noriega-Ortiz
75 Spring Street, 6th floor
New York, New York 10012
212-343-9709
www.bnodesign.com

Peter Dunham
Peter Dunham Design and
Textiles
909 North Orlando Avenue
Los Angeles, California 90069
323-848-9900
www.peterdunham.com

Miles Redd
77 Bleecker Street, Suite C111
New York, New York 10012
212-674-0902
www.milesredd.com

Rose Tarlow
Rose Tarlow-Melrose House
8454 Melrose Place
Los Angeles, California 90069
323-651-2202
www.rosetarlow.com

Ted Russell
1705 Summitridge
Beverly Hills, California 90210
310-275-1609

John Saladino
Saladino Group
200 Lexington Avenue,
Suite 1600
New York, New York 10016
212-684-6805
www.saladinostyle.com

Shawn Hausman
Shawn Hausman Design
1285 North Crescent Heights
Boulevard, Suite L
Los Angeles, California 90046
323-656-0898
www.shawnhausmandesign.com

Kate Stamps
Stamps and Stamps
318 Fairview Avenue
South Pasadena, California 91030
626-441-5600
www.stampsandstamps.com

Stephen Shadley
Stephen Shadley Designs Inc.
144 West 27th Avenue
New York, New York 10001
212-243-6913
www.stephenshadley.com

Andrew Virtue
VIRTUE Interior Design
5318 East 2nd Street, Suite 698
Long Beach, California 90803
562-856-1789
www.virtueinteriors.com

Waldo Fernandez
Waldo's Design
620 North Almont Drive
Los Angeles, California 90069
310-278-1803
www.waldosdesigns.com

First published in the United States of America in 2007
by Rizzoli International Publications, Inc.
300 Park Avenue South
New York, New York 10010
www.rizzoliusa.com

Photography copyright © 2006 Tim Street-Porter

2007 2008 2009 2010 / 10 9 8 7 6 5 4 3 2

PRINTED IN CHINA

ISBN-10: 0-8478-2917-0
ISBN-13: 978-0-8478-2917-0

Library of Congress Control Number: 2006939428

Project Editor: Sandra Gilbert
Art Direction: Doug Turshen + David Huang Design Studio